# LIGHT

*for*

# DARK TIMES

Jeff Crippen
Justice Keepers Publishing
www.unholycharade.com

Edited by Verla Crippen

Cover design by Jessica Brown

Interior design by Verla Crippen & Jessica Brown

Book Layout ©2017 BookDesignTemplates.com

Light for Dark Times: An Arsenal of Truth to Expose Domestic Abuse/ Jeff Crippen. —1st ed.

ISBN: 9780998198132

# LIGHT

## *for*

# DARK TIMES

### AN ARSENAL OF TRUTH TO EXPOSE
### DOMESTIC ABUSE

# JEFF CRIPPEN

*Justice Keepers Publishing*

# CONTENTS

# PREFACE

*"For though we walk in the flesh, we are not waging war according to the flesh. For the weapons of our warfare are not of the flesh but have divine power to destroy strongholds. We destroy arguments and every lofty opinion raised against the knowledge of God, and take every thought captive to obey Christ," (2 Corinthians 10:3-5)*

THIS BOOK IS A KIND OF ARSENAL. Battle armor, you might say, to be used defensively and offensively against evil, and specifically against the evil we call abuse. Here I have put into print form (with the help of several excellent friends) some articles which are taken from my blog, *Unholy Charade* (unholycharade.com). If you follow the blog, you will recognize many of them.

It occurred to me that there are some real advantages to having the articles in the form of a printed book as well as online. Many people prefer a book in hand rather than reading out there in cyber-land, and a book is something that you can easily hand off to a friend or other person who can be helped by what this collection contains. You can underline and dog-ear a book, and grab it quickly to remind yourself or a friend of some paragraph that really helped you. Of course the book is also published in kindle format for people who prefer it on their phone or other device.

There is no particular order to the articles. I could have organized them into sections according to subject headings since many of them address the same or similar nuance of abuse. But in the end, I decided to follow no grouping and provide a table of contents for the reader to use.

This book, as I said, is a kind of arsenal. I hope that it is an arsenal of the Lord's truth and not just my opinions. Blog post topics almost always come to my mind when I am reading the Bible, or when something many of you have written to me turns my thinking toward a particular Scripture. We need such an arsenal to help us wield the Sword the Lord has given us in His Word to be used to expose and destroy the evil weaponry that strives to oppose Christ and His people.

*Unholy Charade* is a blog ministry that exists to expose the evil of domestic abusers hiding behind a "saintly" disguise in churches, and to help the victims of such abusers by helping them see what has been happening to them, teaching them to be wise about this evil, validating them by believing them, and freeing them from the abuser's allies who so often are the victim's fellow church members or leaders. This book is written for the same purposes. May the Lord bless this tool and all who take it up and lead His people safely through the valley of the shadow into freedom.

In Christ,
Jeff, Pastor at Christ Reformation Church
Tillamook, Oregon

# Acknowledgements

I WANT FIRST TO THANK the members of Christ Reformation Church (both here in Tillamook and those who have joined us online) for their constant encouragement to carry on this ministry. We have faced many obstacles together and the Lord has faithfully seen us through them all. Those who have been together with us from the beginning way back in 2010 know with certainty that the Lord is the one who started it all and who has directed us and provided for us at each step.

And many thanks to my wife Verla for her hours of work editing and formatting, to our friend Renee who for years now has worked behind the scenes on the blog. And thank you also to Jessica who we have watched grow up and become a great help to us.

Finally, there are scores (hundreds?) of people I have never seen and yet who have been key in helping us carry on. They are the ones who read our articles and books and recognize the Lord's truth working to set them free from the bondage evil has put upon them. You know them. They are you!

# WOLVES IN WOOL

*"Beware of false prophets, who come to you in sheep's clothing but inwardly are ravenous wolves." (Matt. 7:15)*

*"I know that after my departure fierce wolves will come in among you, not sparing the flock;" (Acts 20:29)*

EVIL HIDES. It is secretive. It wears disguises. It is, after all, of the kingdom of darkness and hates the light. Wolves wear wool. Sheep never put on a wolf's pelt to disguise themselves but wolves wear wool to pass themselves off as one of the flock. This imagery of course is given to us by the Lord Jesus to warn us that wicked people (false teachers, predators, self-glory seekers, abusers and others) are going to do their diabolical best to deceive us. To trick us into believing that they are one of us. That they are servants of Christ, and even eminent servants of the Lord.

*"And no wonder, for even Satan disguises himself as an angel of light. (2 Corinthians 11:14)*

The articles in this book are taken from my blog at Unholy Charade. Consequently, they deal with the evil of domestic abusers and how these wicked ones so often hide in local churches and win the pastors and members as their allies. But by studying the particular evil of the domestic abuser, we can learn much about the other kinds of evil which all strive to gain power and control and glory for themselves.

*"I have written something to the church, but Diotrephes, who likes to put himself first, does not acknowledge our authority. So if I come, I will bring up what he is doing, talking wicked nonsense against us. And not content with that, he refuses to welcome the brothers, and also stops those who want to and puts them out of the church."*
*(3 John 1:9-10)*

Power and control. There it is. The thing is devilish because it is of its father the devil who, you will recall, strives above all to be like the Most High. That was his scheme from the beginning. You see it in his lying words to Eve:

*"For God knows that when you eat of it your eyes will be opened, and you will be like God, knowing good and evil."*
*(Genesis 3:5)*

This craving for deity is really at the very heart of the essence of sin. That is why John calls it lawlessness:

*"Everyone who makes a practice of sinning also practices lawlessness; sin is lawlessness." (1 John 3:4)*

Evil, you see, writes its own law. Its mentality is a profound and unquestioning entitlement *to be God.* The one who sets himself up as god, the one known as the antichrist to come, is named by Paul as "the lawless one." (see 2 Thessalonians 2:3) Therefore, to understand evil, to be wise as serpents about evil, we must begin here. *Evil wants to be God.* And this is why evildoers, like domestic abusers and wolves such as Diotrephes want to be "first" in a church, do what they do. Every word, every action is motivated by this lust for power and control and deity.

The articles in this book are written in the hope that they will help you become wise. So that God's truth will begin to dispel that confusing, blinding "fog" which evildoers like abusers cast over us. Every article necessarily then explores some aspect of this evil quest for godhood. If you are an abuser target, then you can be sure that his (or her) motive at the bottom of it all is *to be God to you.* To demand your worship and service.

*"And whoever does not fall down and worship shall immediately be cast into a burning fiery furnace." (Dan. 3:6)*

When we refuse to worship the false god, we can be confident that the idol and his followers will do their hellish best to put us into some kind of fiery furnace. Slander, blaming, solitary confinement, threats, physical attacks, crazy-making mind games, legal action, economic deprivation, and on and on the list of wicked tactics these kind launch against Christ's people.

I know these things are real. I have experienced them in, of all places, local "Christian" churches and organizations. The very people who professed to be my brothers and sisters in the Lord often turned out to be false brethren. Plants come in among us sent from their infernal father to work destruction among Christ's true people. Many if not most of you who have picked up this book know these things all too well yourselves and the arena of attacks against you has been the same – the local church.

I had to wise up to these things to be free. Rather I suppose I should say, the Lord had to wise me up and He did so by putting me in the lion's den for many years, then kindly showing me the truth of what was really happening. May He use the following articles to do the same enlightening and freeing work in your life too.

# An Unholy Charade
# in the Church

*"For people will be lovers of self, lovers of money, proud, arrogant, abusive, disobedient to their parents, ungrateful, unholy..." (2 Timothy 3:2)*

*"My companion stretched out his hand against his friends; he violated his covenant. His speech was smooth as butter, yet war was in his heart; his words were softer than oil, yet they were drawn swords." (Psalm 55:20-21)*

IF YOU ARE A CHRISTIAN, a genuine, real, child of God regenerated by faith alone in Christ alone, then it is essential that you become wise as serpents regarding the tactics and schemes of your enemy, the Prince of Darkness. Paul told the Corinthians that Satan and his servants come to us in disguise, masking themselves in a charade of false holiness in order to deceive and enslave us. Wise as serpents. Innocent as doves.

But most Christians are not wise. And as result, neither are they innocent because they foolishly become the ally of the wicked in oppressing their victims. This unholy charade is being carried out in the church which Christ calls to be a pillar of His truth!

One of the most common and numerous kinds of these charlatans is the evil man we call *the domestic abuser*. His unholy charade is one of "holy saintliness." Here he is, a "fine" church member, a pastor, a missionary, an elder or deacon, present every

Sunday at his "holiest." He is often the "go to guy" who sacrificially stands ready to help others. He often puts himself forward as a model of fatherhood, ready to instruct others (especially his wife) what a godly wife and mother should look like. At other times, when it is convenient and more profitable to his quest for power and control over his target, this kind of man plays the victim. How he has tried and tried in his marriage, you know. Just ask him! But his wife...well...his wife is, rebellious, difficult, unwilling.

It is all a facade. The domestic abuser (we will normally simply call him the "abuser") in reality is an entirely different man than those folks down at the church think he is. He takes off his disguise behind the scenes. The times he is alone with his wife. In his home or other settings, unseen to those who believe him to be the holiest of the holy. His arsenal of evil tactics, all used toward his primary goal of gaining and maintaining power and control, is very large. And most people have no idea that he is using them, so effective is his ability to deceive.

Many of you who have read my book *Unholy Charade* or my first book, *A Cry for Justice*, know what the standard, typical, widespread experience is of a Christian woman who is married to a domestic abuser. When she finally (we say finally because there are many factors working against her even realizing what is happening to her)...when she finally musters up courage to go to her pastor or other fellow Christians for help, her story does not proceed to "and they all lived happily ever after." Not at all.

Her life takes even more turns for the worse. It gets much worse. With very few exceptions her local church works to keep her in bondage, minimizes the evil she has been enduring for years, and eventually focuses its energy on "fixing" her abuser and "fixing" her marriage. All of this is destined to miserable failure, and when it does all fall apart, the victim will be the scapegoat. "She just didn't trust the Lord. She wouldn't try hard enough."

My purpose in the articles I write is to continue to 1) expose these unholy charlatans hiding in the local church for what they are, and 2) to believe and validate victims, helping them to understand what is happening to them, to identify the false, unbiblical counsel they are receiving, and point them to the freedom that is theirs in Christ.

I invite you to come along with me as we shine Christ's light into the darkness of this evil. This wickedness is in *your* church! I can say that without fear of being wrong. It is a wickedness that is of the most evil, vile and hardened kind. I know of pastors, right at this moment, who are living this unholy charade, preaching from their pulpits every Sunday, giving people "biblical" counsel in their offices, but who in reality are wickedly and habitually abusing their wives behind the scenes. Their flock think that they know him. They do not.

Let's turn up the heat for these creeps who have crept in among us and in so doing see if we cannot also help the targets of their abuse find freedom.

*The people who are secretly practicing evil while playing the game of pretend as good Christians are the hardest and most treacherous of all abusers. When a person decides to use the mask of Christianity for his unholy charade, he commits an odious sin which, if persisted in leads to a final departure of the Lord from him.*

# The Heart and Mind
## of the Abuser

*"I have written something to the church, but Diotrephes,
who likes to put himself first, does not acknowledge our
authority. So if I come, I will bring up what he is doing,
talking wicked nonsense against us. And not content with
that, he refuses to welcome the brothers, and also stops
those who want to and puts them out of the church."
(3 John 1:9-10)*

AT THE HEART AND IN THE MIND of all abusers - be they
domestic, sexual, or spiritual - is this profound mentality of
entitlement to power and control. You see it in this Diotrephes
who the Apostle John is going to take on. Diotrephes "likes to put
himself first." And so it is in an abusive marriage. The abuser is to
be top dog, or else.

This is quite different than mere selfishness. We all have a
streak of that in us. Much of child-rearing entails teaching and
discipline that is designed to teach the child not to be selfish. To
care for others. To be generous and kind. But the abuser is another
creature entirely.

*Entitlement*. There is the key word. Domestic abusers for
instance actually believe that they *deserve* power and control.
They *deserve* to be made the center of the universe. They deserve
to possess. And the flip side of this thinking is that their victim
does NOT deserve - anything. This is the essence of the abuser's
worldview. This is who he is. (or in some cases, who "she" is). Of

course, this no excuse! The Lord holds the wicked accountable for their evils. Diotrephes might be an abuser, but John is going to confront him in front of everyone.

As you begin to understand these things, you are helped. If you are an abuse victim, then you are helped as the truth of what you are dealing with comes into clearer focus. Abusers, you may know, love to keep things foggy. They confuse those around them with their seemingly unpredictable behaviors, with their excuses, with their blaming and what we call "crazy-making." But as Jesus said, and boy is it ever true! - "The truth shall make you free!" "Oh, so THAT's what he has been doing to me!" The lights start to come on.

Those who deal with pedophiles know that *everything a pedophile does is motivated by a desire to have sex with children.* It's an ugly, ugly truth - but there it is in all its stench. The car they buy. The career they choose. The CHURCH they choose. The "friends" they make. All of it and more - everything they do - is done toward that heinous goal.

The mindset of entitlement to power and control in the abuser is what drives and defines him. There seems to be a kind of sliding scale of abuse. Some abusers are apparently worse than others. Nevertheless, they are all defined by this view of themselves and the world. Entitlement. Power. Control. Justification. And therefore, it is their very person who drives them to do what they do. Their schemes and tactics are all used for the same goal - power and control over. Marriage and who they marry. Economic rules they impose. The isolation of their victim that they enforce. The lying. The list goes on and on but just as a football team's entire playlist is designed and practiced with the goal of crossing that end zone line, so the abuser has his wicked playbook.

Are you a pastor, a church leader, a church member? Then you are very foolish if you think that you know all you need to know about this subject. Foolish not only because you don't know much at all about such wicked people who creep in among your flock, but foolish *because if you are a genuine pastor who truly knows*

*Christ and really desire to serve Him, then YOU are being targeted by spiritual abusers like Diotrephes*. I know. I was. And it took years for the lights to come on. They almost drove me out of the ministry I am called to. That church pianist/choir director who rules "her" music kingdom, that elder or deacon who insists that you "come on over to my place on Monday mornings so we can talk about the church," or that Bible class teacher who everyone thinks is just the most wonderful Christian in the world (but who makes it clear you are not going to tell him what to do), all of these characters and more are lusting for the power and control that THEY are entitled to, and to which YOU are a threat. These are not the mere "personality conflicts" with "difficult people" we were told about back in seminary or in the Christian books we read. Oh no. These are emissaries of the kingdom of darkness.

> *"You said in your heart, 'I will ascend to heaven; above the stars of God I will set my throne on high; I will sit on the mount of assembly in the far reaches of the north; I will ascend above the heights of the clouds; I will make myself like the Most High.'" (Isaiah 14:13-14)*

Entitlement. Power. Control. Mark those terms down well. They really explain everything.

# ANOTHER BASIC ATTITUDE IN THE ABUSER - JUSTIFICATION

*"He waited seven days, the time appointed by Samuel. But Samuel did not come to Gilgal, and the people were scattering from him. So Saul said, "Bring the burnt offering here to me, and the peace offerings." And he offered the burnt offering. As soon as he had finished offering the burnt offering, behold, Samuel came. And Saul went out to meet him and greet him. Samuel said, "What have you done?" And Saul said, "When I saw that the people were scattering from me, and that you did not come within the days appointed, and that the Philistines had mustered at Michmash, I said, 'Now the Philistines will come down against me at Gilgal, and I have not sought the favor of the LORD.' So I forced myself, and offered the burnt offering." (1Samuel 13:8-12)*

"I HAD TO DO IT." "I did it for your own good." "You made me do it." These are some examples of the mentality of *justification* which characterize the abuser's thinking. Entitlement to power and control and justification in doing whatever is necessary to obtain and maintain unwarranted, unauthorized, power and control. This statement really defines the abuser.

You see it here in Saul. When confronted by Samuel for offering sacrifices he had no right to offer, Saul blamed first *circumstances* (not his fault) and then he blamed Samuel (again, not his fault). Saul was, in his thinking, *justified* in doing what he did.

And so it goes with the domestic abuser (and other types of abusers too). He rages at his target all evening long until she is beaten down and the children are hiding out of sight. And though later he may bring her flowers, he still believes he was entirely justified in doing this to her. And he will do it again in spite of any promises not to. After all, in the end he was justified in what he did. She needed his raging punishment. Maybe he didn't want to do it, but it had to be done, you know.

This mentality of justification is why the abuser will sleep quite well that night and often act, the next morning, as if the whole thing never happened. Really, he is boosted by what he did. He did what is *right*. He did what he has a *right* to do.

I am no expert on sociopaths and psychopaths, but I suspect that those who are experts would tell us that these conscienceless people are also characterized by this same mindset of justification. The serial killer - somehow what he did was something he was entitled to do. The lady who was city treasurer for a small town some years ago and who embezzled over $50 million dollars over a twenty-year period to finance her elaborate lifestyle - was able to sleep at night and face her victims every day. These people, including domestic abusers, are not sorry. They are not repentant. Because like Saul, what they did *had to be done.*

Why is all this important for us to know? Because unless we understand the mentality of the abuser, *we will fail to prescribe the right remedy!* Victims will keep waiting for him to be sorry, and change. Churches will pressure and demand that victims stay with the abuser, forbidding separation or divorce. After all, their mantra goes, "no one is beyond God's mercy."

But that is not true. The Lord does not show His mercy to the hypocrite who refuses to repent. By his own choice, such a person IS beyond God's mercy. You see this in Christ's words to the Pharisees:

> *"Why do you not understand what I say? It is because you cannot bear to hear my word. You are of your father the devil, and your will is to do your father's desires. He was a murderer from the beginning, and does not stand in the truth, because there is no truth in him. When he lies, he*

*speaks out of his own character, for he is a liar and the father of lies. But because I tell the truth, you do not believe me." (John 8:43-45)*

We must come to understand that the domestic abuser does not think like we do. Until we get hold of this truth, we will continue to be duped by him. We will speak the wrong message to him. We will feel pity and empathy for him and thereby be drawn into his deceiving web.

Let me conclude with an illustration. Many years ago, I knew a fellow who appeared to be down on his luck. He didn't have much income, didn't have a job, and he had a family. He drove an old beat up car that belonged in the junkyard and eventually it gave out on him. One day I went to visit him and found him lying in the snow under that car pulling the transmission out of it for repairs. Pity.

So I said to Mike, as we shall call him, "Mike, what do you say I drive you to town and we buy you a car that runs?" And that is what we did. I bought him a $400 car and it did run! Believe it or not it was a much better set of wheels than what he had been driving.

Now, I didn't have very much money back then myself. And what I did was not wrong. It wasn't stupid. It was an act of kindness. But what I didn't have a clear grasp on was something that a friend told me a few days later. He said, "Jeff, the fact is that you care about Mike's situation more than Mike does." And that was true truth. I thought I knew how Mike must have felt and what he was thinking when I saw him under that car in the snow. I didn't – Mike didn't think like me. I assumed he did.

Your abuser does not think like you do. His mindset is one of *justification*. He is not sorry. He is not repentant. For all the crocodile tears that he might let flow sometimes, he is entitled to power and control over you and he is fully justified in using his arsenal of abuse tactics on you.

It's for your own good, you know.

# PEACE, PEACE, WHEN
# THERE IS NO PEACE

*"Therefore I will give their wives to others and their fields to conquerors, because from the least to the greatest everyone is greedy for unjust gain; from prophet to priest, everyone deals falsely. They have healed the wound of my people lightly, saying, 'Peace, peace,' when there is no peace.'" (Jeremiah 8:10-11)*

AS MANY OF YOU are very much aware, the Lord's words about the wicked false prophets and priests play out in our day all the time as well. I want to show you how you as a target of an abuser can expect to hear this pronouncement from so many of those to whom you turn for help. "Peace, peace" - when in fact there is no peace.

A common response to someone who blows the whistle on evil is what we call "minimization." "You are making a mountain out of a mole hill. Surely it can't be that serious. Everyone has hard times in their marriage. He was just having a bad day. He didn't really mean it." That sort of thing. Taking a very serious evil and watering it down. Minimizing it. And I maintain that this is of the very same spirit as those false prophets Jeremiah faced. "Peace. We have peace with God. All is well. No need to worry yourself. Don't listen to Jeremiah. He's always doom and gloom you know."

But what is the truth? The truth is that there is NO peace with an abuser. Never. Not now. Not ever. There really are people who desire war, and abusers are of that genre. You know it if you are a target of such a man. The cycle of abuse (you can find that cycle diagrammed in most books on abuse or online) ALWAYS is headed toward another round of abuse even while it seems to be in the "peace" mode. Because all that such a false peace is doing is serving up the abuser the ability to dupe his victim into thinking, as he loves to say, "oh, that will never happen again." Or "that never happened, are you crazy? Let's go out on a nice date."

You may have read elsewhere where I have told the story of one of the most evil men and abusers I have ever come across. He caused grief and trouble for decades. But when he was exposed and sent down the road, his pitiable-face response was "but we did have some good times didn't we?" The answer? NO! None. Even in those "peaceful" times his motive was simply to set us up for the next attack.

When you are in a relationship with an abuser, there is no peace. And yet, expect it, you are going to have people around you telling you, in varieties of terms, "peace, peace. All is well. It's ok. Go home and try harder." Don't believe them. Recognize their false message for what it is. Don't believe your abuser when he starts in on another abuse cycle, working to set you up for the next boot-smack.

> *"Trusting in a treacherous man in time of trouble is like a bad tooth or a foot that slips." (Proverbs 25:19)*

Yes, there ARE treacherous men. Do not put your trust in them. All they ever offer is a false peace.

# Angry Tears –
# Don't be Duped

*"And this second thing you do. You cover the LORD's altar with tears, with weeping and groaning because he no longer regards the offering or accepts it with favor from your hand." (Malachi 2:13)*

*"When you spread out your hands, I will hide my eyes from you; even though you make many prayers, I will not listen; your hands are full of blood." (Isaiah 1:15)*

CHECK OUT THIS GREAT DESCRIPTION of "crocodile tears" that I found at Wikipedia:

*Crocodile tears is a false, insincere display of* emotion such as a hypocrite crying fake tears of grief. The phrase derives from an ancient belief that crocodiles shed tears while *consuming their prey, and as such is present in many* modern languages, especially in Europe where it was introduced through Latin.

You find examples throughout Scripture of *unrepentant* people crying and wailing to the Lord because He won't bless them, hear their prayers, or accept their sacrifices. He is not taken in by this pathetic tactic. But deceitful people keep trying anyway, with all too much success.

Recently a lady who had been targeted by an abuser (she was wise enough to spot it and tell him to hit the road) told me that he could turn on the waterworks at will. And then she shared this really wise insight with me:

He reminded me of a little kid weeping and wailing and throwing a tantrum because he didn't get what he wanted.

In other words, she was describing what we can call "angry tears." These fountains of evil are actually *offensive* outbursts of anger - curses emanating from the tear ducts if you will. But they are cunningly disguised as an expression of "hurt," calling for our empathy and pity. "Oh Joe, I am so sorry. I didn't know that telling you your angry rages frighten me would hurt you so badly."

Tears can be turned on and off at will by these deceivers, so don't be taken in. Realize that in fact what you are watching is a childish tantrum designed to punish you. When it comes to repentance, tears without real change of attitude and behavior are only another form of the abuse continuing. Tears of repentance do not originate in anger.

And a word to pastors and church members. I cannot tell you how many times I have had to confront a wicked person only to have them run to others in the church and turn on the tears. "Oh, how mean he was to me!" Yada, yada, yada. But the frustrating thing is that it works so often! People melt. "God forgives you, we must too. You aren't perfect. We are all sinners."

Somehow behind those tears there is a devilish grin. "Got 'em again!" he says, as the crocodile takes another bite.

# ABUSERS FAIL THE TEST
## OF LOVE

*"A new commandment I give to you, that you love one another: just as I have loved you, you also are to love one another. By this all people will know that you are my disciples, if you have love for one another." (John 13:34-35)*

*"If I speak in the tongues of men and of angels, but have not love, I am a noisy gong or a clanging cymbal. And if I have prophetic powers, and understand all mysteries and all knowledge, and if I have all faith, so as to remove mountains, but have not love, I am nothing." (1 Cor. 13:1-2)*

EVERY REAL CHRISTIAN, that is people who have truly been born again, have been taught to love one another by the Spirit of Christ in them. This is our new creation nature in Jesus. His Law is written on our hearts so that it is part of who the new man is. And this is why Jesus and Paul and other biblical authors tell us that love, the real love of Christ, is THE evidence that we know Him. Specifically, this love is love for Christ and love for Christ's people. Certainly we show love toward unbelievers as well in various ways but the real test is a person's response to the Lord and to His people. The "nicest" pagan to be found will eventually cease to be "nice" if pressed in regard to his thoughts on Jesus.

Paul tells the Corinthians that a person can wear the finest most convincing "holy" disguise all they like, *if they do not love then they are phonies.*

Over the years as a pastor I have known hundreds of people who claim to be Christians. But I have known only a remnant who evidenced the true love of Jesus being present within them. The latter were children of God. The rest were not.

If you are in an abusive relationship - domestic, spiritual, or otherwise - then I can assure you that your abuser fails the test of love. Oh sure, the abuser in his setup stage mouths the words "I love you, baby" over and over, unloading flowers and gifts on you. Blah, blah, blah. It is all meaningless. After all, love does not abuse!

> *"They went out from us, but they were not of us; for if they had been of us, they would have continued with us. But they went out, that it might become plain that they all are not of us. But you have been anointed by the Holy One, and you all have knowledge." (1John 2:19-20)*

Now, where have I really seen this test clearly do its work? Answer: *When the victim finally separates from the abuser.* Think carefully. What you see is an incredible coldness. No grief (it is fake if the tears come). No mercy. No sense of loss of a loving spouse. No love, in other words. And - mark this down - YOU must be careful that your love is not projected into his mind or else you will think that he is thinking like you are? Understand?

And finally, here is something that is no fun at all to realize and yet a victim at some point must get hold of it. *The abuser never loved you.* The person you loved, in fact, did not exist. He was a fictional character that he projected to you, but it was fiction. An act. Such people are incapable of love because they do not desire to love. Love requires giving. The abuser wants only to possess.

Start to understand these things and more of the fog the abuser casts will clear away from your eyes and mind.

# ABUSE VICTIMS ARE BEING THROWN TO THE LIONS

*"No temptation has overtaken you that is not common to man. God is faithful, and he will not let you be tempted beyond your ability, but with the temptation he will also provide the way of escape, that you may be able to endure it." (1Corinthians 10:13)*

THIS PASSAGE OF SCRIPTURE is often misapplied to keep victims of domestic abusers in bondage. However, in this post I want to focus upon God's promise of "the way of escape." Obviously, it is God's will that when we are in a trial or test and we see a way of escape, we take it! After all, God Himself provides it!

Now, there are people who claim to be Christians who will tell you that it is always better (and in fact that God requires it) to remain in the trial. Even "unto death." In other words, they promote martyrdom. Of course they are characterized by the ever-present double standard of the abuser. No way would they become a martyr, but you are required to be one.

Years ago, there was just such a fellow in our church. He was all the time talking about martyrs. Missionary martyrs. Fox's book of the martyrs of church history. And when someone was suffering, he was always right there to say something like - "just submit. This is the Lord's will for you. Just think how great your reward will be." Apparently, he disregarded Jesus' rebuke of the devil. We are forbidden to put the Lord to the test.

Most local churches, pastors, "biblical" counselors, and church members approach domestic abuse in their midst in this very way.

They forbid divorce, and often even forbid separation. You know the routine. It is very common that they tell the victim not to ever call the police. She is to suffer. She is to suffer silently. Otherwise she doesn't have faith, and you know, her abuser's salvation (if they even acknowledge he isn't saved) depends on her, right? This all is nothing less than promoting martyrdom. Requiring the victim to be a martyr. We have known more than one account of the response by a local church in which the victim was murdered by her abuser to be something like: "In the end they are all free now and in heaven together."

In the history of the church there were people, in times of intense persecution, who actively tried to become martyrs. The church had to stop them and make it clear that if God providentially allowed a Christian to be martyred, that was His doing. But to set oneself up intentionally for martyrdom was wrong. If there were a way of escape, a Christian should take it.

And so it is today. Or at least, that is how it should be.

When your pastor or church or some "Christian" book you are reading tells you that God requires you to remain in a marriage to an abuser, they are in fact throwing you to the lions in an arena of their own making. What they are saying is, "You must be a martyr." And often they will remind you, "You know the Bible says":

*"In your struggle against sin you have not yet resisted to the point of shedding your blood." (Hebrews 12:4)*

"So get back out there to the arena and let the lions do what they may. Exit doors may be wide open, but you are not permitted to take them," they say.

No one has a right to throw you to the lions. No one. God is in the business of providing a way of escape. Don't ever be afraid to use it.

# SOME BASIC TRUTHS ABOUT
# ABUSERS AND ABUSE

THE FOLLOWING IS TAKEN in part from my book, *A Cry For Justice*. Please read carefully and you will learn that domestic violence and abuse are far, far more than "wife battering," or some difficult guy who gets drunk on Saturday nights. This evil is much more devilishly sophisticated than that:

In all of its forms, what are the fundamental elements present? Let's define it.

Please understand that abusers may be men or women, but for reasons of simplicity and because more commonly it is the man who is the abuser, we will use "he/him" to refer to the abuser. I have, in fact, known numerous abusers who were women. But the fact remains, the majority are men.

To review, abuse is fundamentally a mentality of *entitlement* and superiority which uses many different tactics to obtain and enforce the *power* and *control* the abuser deems himself entitled to. The abuser judges himself to be absolutely *justified* in using whatever tactics are necessary to ensure this power and control over his victim.

Abuse is effected in many ways: both physical (including sexual) and non-physical (verbal). It can be active (physically or verbally) or passive (not speaking, not acting). Abuse, therefore, is not limited to physical assault. Indeed, the non-physical forms of abuse often are far more damaging, deceptive, and cruel.

Mark these defining terms down very, very carefully. An abuser is a person whose mentality, mindset, and even worldview is dominated by –

- Power

- Control

- Entitlement (to that control)

- Justification (in enforcing that control)

This means that, as I learned, *it is a serious mistake to assume an abuser thinks like everyone else does.* Abuse is rooted in a unique mentality. Any method of dealing with the abuser and helping his victim is destined to failure unless we recognize this fundamental fact. Abusers *are not like you and me. They do not look at other people as we do, nor do they view themselves in ways that we would call "normal."*

Another characteristic of the abuser is his impaired *conscience.* It may even be non-existent (which would classify him as a sociopath). Abuse seems to increase as the functionality of the conscience decreases. Without a conscience, a person cannot engage in meaningful, healthy interpersonal relationships. He cannot *empathize* with others (feel what they feel, understand what they think).

The abuser is the center of his universe. He views his victims as *objects owned by him* to serve him. A person with no empathy nor conscience obviously will *objectify* others – make them into a kind of non-human – and this makes it easier for him to use and abuse them. Because his worldview is one of *entitlement and superiority*, he *minimizes, excuses, and blames others for* the wicked things he says and does to his victim. After all, in his evaluation of the thing, he is *absolutely justified* in doing "what a man has to do" to keep his property in line.

Abusers have a degraded view of women. This is often revealed in the vile, demeaning language they use toward their victim and also in other activities such as the use of pornography. They view women as the enemy, out to get them, always conspiring and conniving to put a man down.

*Raging* is another common tactic of the abuser. Often it comes in the form of a "surprise attack" for no apparent reason. He can be getting something out of the refrigerator, for example, and suddenly start shouting and cursing and throwing things. Raging can go on for quite some time while the victim cowers, fearing for her safety. I remember having an elementary teacher who raged. I was in the 4th grade and Mrs. Hale would suddenly, maybe once each month or so, launch into a shouting tirade against the entire class of nine-year olds. It went on for quite some time. Afterwards, as with most abuser blowups, there would be a kind of "make-up" phase in which she was extra nice to us. Abusers who rage, however, are probably not really out of control, as we might think. If they smash things for example, they often do so selectively – saving their own property.

Remember, power and control is what it is all about. Abusers are not just guys with short tempers who happen to be relational "jerks." They are far more calculated and intentional than that. *They know what they are doing*, and they do it for a definite purpose.

> *"Remember Frodo, the Ring wants to be found."*
> *(Gandalf, Lord of the Rings)*

One way we know this is true is from the masks they wear. They wear their nice-guy mask when it is beneficial for them to do so and reveal who they really are in more secretive settings where there are no outside witnesses. That reeks of intentionality.

That is only a very brief introduction to the abuser mindset and arsenal of tactics. For a much fuller treatment, please read *A Cry for Justice* and *Unholy Charade*. You can order them on Amazon.

# A REAL STORY OF HOW ABUSERS DECEIVE US

THE FOLLOWING IS TAKEN from the third chapter (pp 63-4) of my book, *A Cry for Justice (2012)*. This event happened to me way back in 1982 when I was a police officer in the Portland, Oregon area. (In the story below I am the officer who stayed with Judy, the victim). Myself and a second officer responded to a domestic disturbance call, and this is what happened –

> The church has been failing victims. Pastors and church members, so susceptible to deception because of their ignorance of the abuser's motives, tactics and mentality, become the evil man's ally. Christ's church becomes a place of suffering for the victim. Those who are commissioned by Christ to seek justice end up on the villain's side.
>
> Jared married Judy twelve years ago. They are both members of Christ Evangelical Church and are well thought of. Jared is particularly active, serving on two committees, one of which he chairs. But today, Jared is in jail.
>
> Last night, Judy called the police after Jared twisted her arm. He has done this before, but this time he went too far and broke it. When the police arrived, Jared was standing in the yard to greet them, cool and calm. One officer stayed with him while the other went inside. Judy was sitting on the couch dressed only in her underwear, holding her arm. The officer gave her a blanket to cover up and asked her what had happened. Jared, she said, often gets violent and this time had actually broken her arm. She felt it break and heard it snap. Judy was sobbing.

While waiting for the ambulance, the officer with her looked out the front window. Jared was still speaking calmly with his partner, even laughing about some joke. The officer turned back to Judy and asked her again what had happened. "I told you. He broke my arm."

Still battling with feelings of disbelief – "this guy is so calm and even jovial" – the officer went back outside and confronted Jared. "She's crazy! I have no idea how her arm was injured. I came home from work, ate dinner, and later she came running out of the hallway yelling that her arm was broken." But the fresh scratch marks on Jared's forearms told a different story. The officers arrested Jared and transported him to jail. If it hadn't been for those scratches....?

Jared was trying, almost successfully, to win the police as his allies. He was telling jokes about the fickleness of women, plying on men's common struggles with the female sex, and so on. Before this all sorts itself out, Jared will win numbers of his fellow church members over to his side. Judy will be chastised for causing him so much trouble. Why couldn't she just let bygones be bygones. What of the children? Now their daddy is in jail! And if Judy leaves Jared (which she should!), Jared will become a victim to be pitied by the rest of the church as Christians quote "God hates divorce," – a phrase, incidentally, that is not really in the Bible. Check Malachi 2:16 in the ESV for confirmation.

# A COMMON CLAIM -
# "ONLY GOD CAN JUDGE"

*"For what have I to do with judging outsiders? Is it not those inside the church whom you are to judge? God judges those outside. 'Purge the evil person from among you.'" (1 Corinthians 5:12-13)*

I WAS READING A COMMENTARY on Matthew this morning and came across the following statement by the author:

> God is the one truly competent Judge, for he alone knows all things. Every human judgment is based on imperfect knowledge. We make every decision on insufficient evidence. Not so with God. He knows all that is, was, and shall be.[1]

Now, this statement is true, in part at least. God is indeed the only truly competent judge. He is the only one who knows all things. This cannot be said of any human. If perfection in judgment is the subject of discussion, yes - it is only to be found in God.

However...

If you have been or currently are the target of a domestic abuser, sociopath, narcissist, or other generally evildoer, you have probably had this kind of statement thrown at you to keep you quiet. "Only God is able to judge." "You cannot judge because you do not know that person's heart." Judge not. Yada, yada, yada.

What is conveniently omitted from such claims of course are the many verses in Scripture, such as the one quoted above, that

---

[1] *Matthew: Reformed Expository Commentary*, Daniel Doriani

not only tell us we can judge another person, but that we *must* do so. Here is another in the very next chapter of 1 Corinthians:

*"When one of you has a grievance against another, does he dare go to law before the unrighteous instead of the saints? Or do you not know that the saints will judge the world? And if the world is to be judged by you, are you incompetent to try trivial cases? Do you not know that we are to judge angels? How much more, then, matters pertaining to this life! So if you have such cases, why do you lay them before those who have no standing in the church? I say this to your shame. Can it be that there is no one among you wise enough to settle a dispute between the brothers," (1Corinthians 6:1-5)*

The implication, which is entirely illogical, in the "only God is competent to judge" nonsense is that *perfect knowledge is required in order to make a judgement.* But clearly it is not required:

*"A healthy tree cannot bear bad fruit, nor can a diseased tree bear good fruit. Every tree that does not bear good fruit is cut down and thrown into the fire. Thus you will recognize them by their fruits." (Matthew 7:18-20)*

I do not need to know everything that is possible to know about apple trees before I can make a very judgmental statement: "This is a very bad apple." It really isn't true that my judgment of a bad apple is based on "imperfect knowledge" as this commentator claims. While my knowledge may be *incomplete* as to the total knowledge of apples, the data I have is accurate. That is a wormhole. This apple is small and scaly and flavorless. Those are perfectly true observations and they lead me to a perfectly true judgment - bad apple.

If perfectly complete knowledge of some person or event in our universe were required before a judgment could be made, thus leaving God the only one able to judge, consider the implications:

- Civil courts would have to be closed because reaching a verdict would be impossible

- I could not make any judgments based upon my observations - "that is a good sound car. I am going to buy it."

- Science, in fact, would have to be discarded.

- Knowledge, in other words, would be impossible for human beings.

- Morality and law would necessarily be null and void. After all, discerning what is right and wrong requires making a judgment.

This kind of thinking, as bizarre as it may sound, is actually permeating our world today. "You cannot judge what the United States Constitution really means because that is a judgment. We just have to make it a fluid, changing, adapting document which develops as time rolls on." We are seeing the chaos and insanity in which such thinking results.

So, the next time some pastor or counselor or fellow Christian pulls this "we are not competent to judge" card on you, well... laugh at them. "What did you just say? Only God is able to judge? We are not able to judge that a person is evil? Is that what you said?" And then go right on seeing clearly that your abuser is indeed an evil person. Make your decisions - your judgments - based upon that sound truth.

# PRAYING FOR GOD'S JUSTICE

*"Arise, O LORD; O God, lift up your hand; forget not the afflicted. Why does the wicked renounce God and say in his heart, 'You will not call to account'? But you do see, for you note mischief and vexation, that you may take it into your hands; to you the helpless commits himself; you have been the helper of the fatherless. Break the arm of the wicked and evildoer; call his wickedness to account till you find none. The LORD is king forever and ever; the nations perish from his land. O LORD, you hear the desire of the afflicted; you will strengthen their heart; you will incline your ear to do justice to the fatherless and the oppressed, so that man who is of the earth may strike terror no more." (Psalm 10:12-18)*

FORGIVENESS. Reconciliation. Love. Mercy. Justice? How does that last one fit into our Christian experience? Jesus said we are to love our enemies and pray for those who persecute us. Maybe the prayers of Psalm 10 are Old Testament stuff, not for us today? Maybe the same applies to all of those other Psalm-prayers that we call imprecatory?

Wrong!

*Because God has never changed and never will change; His justice, wrath, and judgment against the wicked still stands. In fact, it is increasing in its intensity as evil men oppress His people.*

Let me prove it with a NEW Testament imprecatory prayer –

*"Therefore we ourselves boast about you in the churches of God for your steadfastness and faith in all your persecutions and in the afflictions that you are enduring. This is evidence of the righteous judgment of God, that you may be considered worthy of the kingdom of God, for which you are also suffering – since indeed God considers it just to repay with affliction those who afflict you, and to grant relief to you who are afflicted as well as to us, when the Lord Jesus is revealed from heaven with his mighty angels in flaming fire, inflicting vengeance on those who do not know God and on those who do not obey the gospel of our Lord Jesus. They will suffer the punishment of eternal destruction, away from the presence of the Lord and from the glory of his might, when he comes on that day to be glorified in his saints, and to be marveled at among all who have believed, because our testimony to you was believed." (2 Thessalonians 1:4-10)*

Pretty tough words, right? When a victim of abuse comes to us for help, we need to tell them about the wrath and judgment of God that is set against the evil happening to them! We do not need to preach to victims about how they need to be kind to their abuser, how they need to love him, how they need to forgive him and submit to him...blah, blah, blah.

We are not denying that the Christian is to love his enemies and do good to his persecutors as he has opportunity, not seeking personal vengeance. But victims need the encouragement and affirmation from us that God is FOR them, and that He is AGAINST their abuser. And we need to stand by these victims and assure them that WE are for them as well! I suggest that it is very appropriate to sit down with an abuse victim, open our Bible up to an imprecatory prayer Psalm like Psalm 10, and pray through it with the victim! We almost seem to think today in our Christian circles that to do such a thing is sinful!

Have we tamed God? Maybe in our minds. But in reality, He is the same consuming fire He always has been, and as such is to be feared with a terrorizing fear by any person who would dare oppress His people, His bride.

# 13

# WHY THE "CHRISTIAN" ABUSER IS THE WORST KIND

*"Pay careful attention to yourselves and to all the flock, in which the Holy Spirit has made you overseers, to care for the church of God, which he obtained with his own blood. I know that after my departure fierce wolves will come in among you, not sparing the flock; and from among your own selves will arise men speaking twisted things, to draw away the disciples after them. Therefore be alert, remembering that for three years I did not cease night or day to admonish everyone with tears." (Acts 20:28-31)*

I THINK THAT CHRISTIANS are faced with the worst kind of abuser – the "Christian" abuser. The person who claims to be a Christian but who is nothing but a facade and who, in reality, is a power and control motivated, entitlement-thinking wolf in wool. And it is important for us to realize this. Not only are we often the most naive people when it comes to "getting it" about abuse, but we in the Christian church often have to face the most evil abusers.

Why do I suggest this?

Well, just consider what is required for a person to be an abuser and then in addition, play out his abuse in the charade of a Christian character. Surely we must see that this kind of act requires a much harder heart and lack of conscience than doing the same thing "out there" in the world. Notice that the Lord Jesus and the Apostle Paul both called wicked, abusive people within the visible church "wolves." Does the Bible call any enemies of Christ who are outside the visible church by this same title? Maybe I have missed such a Scripture passage, but I can't think of one. A wolf who dons a sheep's disguise and sneaks in among the flock is a far greater danger and of a greater savagery than one that makes no pretense to be anything but what he is, a wolf.

So what does this mean for Christians? It means that of all people on this planet, we are the ones who need to be and who should be the real experts on the nature, mentality, and tactics of evil. We should know these things better than anyone else. Because we are the ones who are going to have to face the greatest threat and the most cunning representatives of the enemy. Right now, it does not seem to be so. What we see over and over again is the most ill-prepared soldiers facing the craftiest agents of evil. The result is that we are duped, victims suffer even more because of our ineptitude, and the enemy must be really enjoying himself watching all of it.

The fact that an abuser who is a professing Christian is the worst kind of abuser also has implications for victims and for those who would help those victims. A woman, for example, whose husband is of this sort is facing an even more intensified degree of abuse. Why? Because, let me say it once more, being wicked and at the same time choosing to masquerade as a Christian requires a greater degree of evil. The raging abuser whose violence is plain to see may look far worse than the nice, respectable, saintly fellow we know at church and yet who is a demon at home. But think it through. Which one of the two is called a "wolf" by Christ?

The Word of God very often points to evil people who sneak in among the church as particular dangers. For example:

> *"These are hidden reefs at your love feasts, as they feast with you without fear, shepherds feeding themselves; waterless clouds, swept along by winds; fruitless trees in late autumn, twice dead, uprooted; wild waves of the sea, casting up the foam of their own shame; wandering stars,*

*for whom the gloom of utter darkness has been reserved forever." (Jude 1:12-13)*

Where in God's Word do we find that level of intense condemnation for someone who is outside the visible church, making no claim of Christ at all? It does seem that Scripture agrees with us then when we suggest that as Christians, we can expect to face the most evil kind of abuser.

And that fact alone should be enough to make us all sit up and take notice that maybe, just maybe, these victims who come to us for help just might be telling us the truth.

# 14

# WILL YOUR CHURCH
# STAND WITH YOU?

WITH SOME REGULARITY I hear from people who tell me that they are on board with this issue of domestic abusers hiding in the church. They are excited that their pastor has "really had his eyes opened" and is "promising to stand with abuse victims." And I have heard the same from various well-known Christian counseling ministries.

I don't believe most of them. And when I say so, let me tell you, I lose friends and I do not gain any popularity with the "happening" crowds in Christendom. They accuse me of being narrow and arrogant, as if "only I know anything."

But the truth is, I do know that they still cannot be trusted to stand with victims of abuse. How do I know, you ask? I will tell you. Three things. There are just three things that you need to find out - and then you will know too. Ready? [If they fail at any ONE of these, they fail all]

1.  **Does this pastor/counselor/church freely acknowledge that abuse is grounds for divorce?** Or do you discern that even if they don't come right out and say "God hates divorce" (not in the Bible by the way), nevertheless they will only talk about "separation" for abuse. I have found that pastors and counselors and so-called experts on domestic abuse dance all around the D-I-V-O-R-C-E word.

2.  **Does this pastor/counselor/church freely permit an abuse victim to decide *for herself* to divorce her abuser,** or will they be upset if she decides that she does not want to be married to this abuser and files for

divorce? In other words, do they indicate that she must have their permission to divorce?

3. **Does this pastor/counselor/church inject themselves into her life and marriage**, insisting that she allow them to "shepherd" her by counseling the abuser, counseling her, and in general working to "redeem" the marriage and fix the abuser?

If any one of these elements is present in your pastor or church leaders then you can be sure that in the end, *they will not stand with you.* Oh they can be soooo nice and sound soooooo loving and supportive, UNTIL it gets right down to the wire, your abuser has not changed, their fix efforts have failed (as they always will) and you announce you are filing for divorce. So save yourself much grief by finding the answer to these questions early on. And watch out for hesitation and stammering when they give an answer. Don't accept halfway answers.

# 15

# THE ABUSER AS REVILER

*"How long, O God, is the foe to scoff? Is the enemy to revile your name forever." (Psalm 74:10)*

*"Blessed are you when others revile you and persecute you and utter all kinds of evil against you falsely on my account." (Matthew 5:11)*

*"But now I am writing to you not to associate with anyone who bears the name of brother if he is guilty of sexual immorality or greed, or is an idolater, reviler, drunkard, or swindler – not even to eat with such a one." (1 Corinthians 5:11)*

*"Or do you not know that the unrighteous will not inherit the kingdom of God? Do not be deceived: neither the sexually immoral, nor idolaters, nor adulterers, nor men who practice homosexuality, nor thieves, nor the greedy, nor drunkards, nor revilers, nor swindlers will inherit the kingdom of God." (1 Corinthians 6:9-10)*

I WANT US TO THINK about this word "revile" and the person who is called a "reviler" in Scripture. Every abuser is a reviler. As you can see from just these verses, a reviler is not a Christian. Revilers will not inherit the kingdom of God. That is about as plain a way of stating it as you could want.

Reviling is a very, very evil and serious sin. What does it mean? Well, you see that root in there – "vil" – that makes us think about other words like "vilify," or "villain." Revile means to falsely accuse, to malign, to wrongly curse, to make an innocent person the villain. All of you who have been targeted by an abuser know exactly what this looks and feels like. Revilers are the children of the devil. After all, he is known as the accuser of the brethren, right? You even see in the verse from the Psalms quoted above that revilers revile God!

Alright then, what does this reviling look like when it comes our way? I can tell you, and I know that most of you can tell us as well. The reviler looks for opportunity to falsely accuse his victim. One of the most wicked I have ever dealt with (a man who hid behind a facade of "saintliness") seemed to be very unpredictable. You never knew where he would come down on an issue. But eventually we realized that in fact he was very predictable and consistent. He would always be watching for some situation or topic which he could use to vilify others. He would do this by:

- Championing the opposite position, accusing those who saw things otherwise as being wrong or even sinful.

- Watching for a statement or action made by his target, then accusing them of being guilty of sinning for making that statement or performing that action.

- Even more deceitfully, he would "refuse" to voice his opinion or position on a subject, claiming he would simply remain "neutral," when in fact his behavior made a loud and clear statement which accused others of sinning or at least of being seriously wrong.

This is the reviler in action. I have no doubt that local churches are peppered with these kind. Of course, like all abusers, what they are about is fulfilling their lust for power and control, of being "first" and of demanding that everyone does what they say. Diotrephes was a reviler:

*"I have written something to the church, but Diotrephes, who likes to put himself first, does not acknowledge our authority. So, if I come, I will bring up what he is doing,*

*talking wicked nonsense against us. And not content with that, he refuses to welcome the brothers, and also stops those who want to and puts them out of the church."*
*(3 John 1:9-10)*

See it? He lusted to be "first" and to do that he reviled. He vilified. He spoke "wicked nonsense" against the Apostles and other servants of the Lord. Diotrephes was a wolf in wool. John was going to call him out in front of everyone, and that is precisely what we need to do today.

These kind creep into our churches. They crave to be pastors, elders, or "eminent" church members. Their tongue is their weapon of choice.

Now, let me tell you the mistake that genuine Christians often make when they are not yet wise about the reviler. When they are reviled, they accept the guilt, wear the blame, or at minimum they assume that a Christian is to be humble when falsely accused. And sometimes that is the course we are to take. But not when dealing with a reviler. When we see a pattern of reviling in someone, we must realize what we are dealing with is incredibly wicked and is being carried out by a person who is a servant of the devil. We are to put them out of the church and have nothing to do with them.

So then, why is it that pastors and churches and counselors and theologians are telling us otherwise? Why are revilers being warmly received in the church and their victims expelled?

# 16

# A SURE SIGN OF A BULLY
## OR ABUSER

*"Now when they heard these things they were enraged, and they ground their teeth at him." (Acts 7:54)*

RECENTLY I WAS REMINDED still once more of how the wicked react when their evil is exposed and they are called to account. The fangs come out. The bullying begins. They are like vicious, wild animals snapping at their prey. In this account here in Acts 7, Stephen has just confronted the Jews with their sins:

*"You stiff-necked people, uncircumcised in heart and ears, you always resist the Holy Spirit. As your fathers did, so do you. Which of the prophets did your fathers not persecute? And they killed those who announced before-hand the coming of the Righteous One, whom you have now betrayed and murdered." (Acts 7:51-52)*

It sets them off like a pack of wolves and of course as we know, they murdered Stephen right there.

My recent experience with this sort was in regard to pastors who were rightly confronted with wickedness and spiritual abuse. They added to the oppression of victims and now it has come out. The response? Fangs. Gnashing of teeth. Direct assault against those exposing them. Vilification and reviling, demeaning and accusing. Of course, they do all this in the name of "righteousness," but they are anything but righteous. "Who are YOU to tell ME?" "How DARE you speak to me this way." "You don't know anything and I do." "YOU are the guilty one here for slandering and gossiping." See it? Fangs. Gnashing. It is characteristic of the wicked who are enraged when they are exposed. No hint of anything resembling repentance.

When a person, especially someone who claims to be "righteous" and who is in some kind of position of authority, responds in this characteristic manner, you can be sure you are dealing with at best a bully and perhaps even a sociopathic abuser. I am not certain, for that matter, if there is really a difference between the bully and the abuser.

If you look at Scripture and search under "gnashing of teeth" here are some things you come up with:

> *"The wicked plots against the righteous and gnashes his teeth at him" (Psalm 37:12)*

> *"But at my stumbling they rejoiced and gathered; they gathered together against me; wretches whom I did not know tore at me without ceasing; like profane mockers at a feast, they gnash at me with their teeth." (Psalm 35:15-16)*

> *"All your enemies rail against you; they hiss, they gnash their teeth, they cry: 'We have swallowed her! Ah, this is the day we longed for; now we have it; we see it!'" (Lamentations 2:16)*

Pretty cool, huh? By that I mean, it is so revealing of what a person really is because this reaction is so consistent in the wicked. How many times have we seen pastors and writers and leaders of "notoriety" respond in just this way when their sin is put before them? They ooze hatred. They threaten. They demean and accuse. Oh, and often they throw in some words of "piety" as a cover.

Do they literally grind and gnash their teeth? Apparently in some cases yes, they do. Their jaw is clenched. They set their teeth together and scowl hatred. They rail and rage through tightly clenched teeth. And they do this most intensely WHEN THEY KNOW they are busted. The truth is out. It is a murderous thing.

Incidentally then, we must rightly interpret this gnashing of teeth business in Scripture. Haven't we often thought that when the Bible says the wicked will be gnashing their teeth when the Lord consigns them to hell that this teeth-gnashing business is an expression of their anguish and pain? I think that is wrong and misses the point. Gnashing of teeth in the Bible is an expression of hatred, of intense disdain, of "I want to kill you" mentality. With that in mind, consider these verses –

> *"I tell you, many will come from east and west and recline at table with Abraham, Isaac, and Jacob in the kingdom of heaven, while the sons of the kingdom will be thrown into the outer darkness. In that place there will be weeping and **gnashing of teeth.**" (Mathew 8:11-12)*

> *"The Son of Man will send his angels, and they will gather out of his kingdom all causes of sin and all law-breakers, and throw them into the fiery furnace. In that place there will be weeping and **gnashing of teeth**." (Matthew 13:41-42)*

> *"But when the king came in to look at the guests, he saw there a man who had no wedding garment. And he said to him, 'Friend, how did you get in here without a wedding garment?' And he was speechless. Then the king said to the attendants, 'Bind him hand and foot and cast him into the outer darkness. In that place there will be weeping and **gnashing of teeth**.'" (Matthew 22:11-13)*

See it? Don't feel sorry for these characters. Even as they go down to hell, they want to murder Christ! They are beasts, and thus it is appropriate that they are led by a beast –

> *"And I saw the beast and the kings of the earth with their armies gathered to make war against him who was sitting on the horse and against his army. And the beast was captured, and with it the false prophet who in its presence had done the signs by which he deceived those who had received the mark of the beast and those who worshiped its*

*image. These two were thrown alive into the lake of fire that burns with sulfur." (Revelation 19:19-20)*

I say again then, one of the consistent marks of a wolf in sheep's clothing is that when cornered, when confronted with the light of truth, the wool comes off and the wolf comes out. By that I mean that the "pious and godly" church leaders, the noted Christian conference speaker, the saintliest saint in the local church who is in truth a wicked person, will, when pressed with exposure, gnash their teeth. The bullying language and posturing will begin. When that happens, you can be sure that you are dealing with a child of the beast, not with a child of King Jesus.

*"He committed no sin, neither was deceit found in his mouth. When he was reviled, he did not revile in return; when he suffered, **he did not threaten,** but continued entrusting himself to him who judges justly." (1Pet. 2:22-23)*

# 17

# Most of You Have Seen
# Letters Like This

The following is a transcription of a hand-written letter received by one of our blog followers, an abuse survivor. Abused by her abuser and, so typical, by her church as well. The letter was anonymous except of course to claim it is from a fellow Christian "who loves" the victim and her family, including her abuser. I will refer to the letter-writer as "her" because the writing looks to be by a female hand. Here you go. Note it is addressed to the victim AND the abuser. After all, you know, marriage "troubles" are ALWAYS 50-50 shared blame (sarcasm intended). (I have bold-faced terms in the letter which the writer underlined) –

Dear _____ & _____

I want to start by saying, I love you guys!

I would also like to clunk your heads together!

So I propose a few questions, and insights with (illegible),

If either of you had a broken bone, would you go to the doctor? Would you get a cast or brace? Therapy on that body part to make it be back to the most strength possible?

If you had cancer (which may God graciously forbid) would you have surgery to remove it? Radiology? Chemo?

If you had a heart attack, would you have stints or a bypass? Change your diet? Exercise?

Of course you would!

You are two, intelligent, hard-working believers! You both profess you love the Lord! Now it's time to Trust Him! Therefore, let's cut the crap! Let's stop playing 5th grade 'he said,' 'she said.' You have both made some horrific choices. We ALL have! But whatever you have been doing these past 2 years, IS NOT working! The way I see it, you're both incredibly selfish, full of pride and childish!

Yes - no denying some terrible inexcusable things have happened. For this, I AM SO SORRY!

But - here is what I know. Your 3 beautiful children are watching you! They are the real sufferers here. You are doing them a huge disservice. Your actions & how you treat each other is impacting them - and WILL - the rest of their lives. Time to move forward, and forgive!

Marriage is tough - 2 sinners living together, raising more sinners. Divorce - separation is worse than death! This is a personal thing for me, and a real experience. This is what your teaching your kids. Come on guys. REALLY?

I'm not asking you to 'get back together,' right now...but it's time to **Work**! You are both a HOT MESS! But, can you dig deep, for your children? I will not give up on you two!

I am so thankful your issues were brought to light. I will not pick a side - from my own experience I pick your **kids**! **Be sorry**, be humble, be honest! Be sorry! Truly sorry! Please don't take the road of hate! God put you together, he gave you 3 beautiful gifts. It's time to move forward. Get the help needed. I am **pleading** with you to get intense marriage counseling. You can yell, scream, and get it all out. At the minimum, TRY!

If you do this, and then there is no hope, well, I'll be sad! I know there is hope. Please have FAITH in God that there is.

It's time! Your kids need you both! Start being honest with each other. God forgives ALL! Not trying - is lack of faith in God. You cannot show fruits without this faith.

-Matthew 8:26 'And he saith unto them, 'Why are ye fearful, O ye of little faith? Then he arose, and rebuked the winds, and the sea; and there was A GREAT CALM.'

-2 Chronicles 7:14 'If my people which are called by my name shall humble themselves, and pray, and seek my face, and turn from their wicked ways, then will I hear from heaven, and will forgive their sin, and will heal their land.'

You guys are healable! **HAVE FAITH!** We love you - we are here for you **both**! We pray continually for your family! Please, please, please go together to counseling! The Ravines** is a good start! Get the tools needed to be together. Love, _____

   ** Asterisks are mine. I found this quote about the Ravines Retreat Center online. No way do I ever recommend these kinds of things to people, let alone sending an abuse victim and her abuser to this nonsense!

"The Ravines is a retreat center for marriages in crisis and for those who have lost their focus – where marriage struggles have become too much to bear. The Ravines offers Christian intensive marriage counseling to help couples pick up the pieces of their broken (or breaking) relationship, creating a deeper and closer marriage.

We provide a three-day Couples Counseling Intensive experience where couples can find hope, healing and restoration in their relationship. Couples receive Christ-centered therapy in a private setting and are given the uninterrupted time needed to work through difficult and painful issues."

You all can no doubt see how, at best, *stupid* this lady is and most likely, how *arrogant and self-exalting she is.* Her letter is a typical formula for an abuse victim getting deeper and deeper into bondage. Just a few points which you have all probably seen for yourself:

- The letter begins and ends with a claim of "love." "I love you guys!" This statement is a cover for the blasts that are about to follow in the letter. All is excusable because, you know, she says it in "love."

- Notice the amazing number of exclamation marks, all-caps, and underlining. The letter really is written in an assaultive "I would like to clunk your heads together!" mindset.

- She has NO (oops, all caps) idea of what abuse is. None. To her, there is only one problem in any marriage – a two-way shared blame street of selfish-ness and poor communication.

- Her theology is anti-biblical. She insists that Christians are all still sinners, she denies that God's wrath is on anyone, she insists that there is "hope" for everyone. In other words, there was hope for Pharaoh back in the Exodus days. I guess he just needed to go to the counseling center. "God forgives all." Nope. No, He doesn't. That is why there is a hell.

- She prescribes couple's counseling while having no real idea of the abuse that is going on.

- She thinks that all husbands and wives are sinners and that therefore marriage is always tough, but never is it anything that can't be fixed in a 3-day "intensive." I hate that term. "Intensive." Intensive terror is what it is.

- She is very, very accusatory. She throws the dart of lack of faith, of selfishness, of childishness, and more.

- For her, staying in a marriage is always the best for the children. She insists that an abuse victim (though she doesn't even know about abuse) must remain in the marriage for the children's well-being no matter what.

- And did you notice this statement? "Yes - no denying some terrible inexcusable things have happened. For this, I AM SO SORRY!" Now, just what is she talking about? I suspect this means she (and probably the whole church) *is aware of some of the abuse that the abuser has perpetrated on the victim!* And she says that what she knows about is "terrible and inexcusable." She is "sorry" that this happened, but nevertheless the victim is to forgive and forget and return.

- Anonymous. Why? How dare anyone say these kinds of things, intrude into someone's personal life, and then refuse to identify themselves?

In the everyday affairs of life, it is illegal to impersonate a medical doctor. You can't just hang a shingle out and tell people you are a doctor, start seeing patients, and prescribing medications and treatments. But in the church! Well, here is this lady announcing that she knows. She knows the problems and she knows the answers. Not surprising that her prescriptions will result in disaster, increased suffering, ruined lives, and even death.

I don't know if this lady will ever see this post, but in the off-chance that she does - "Madam, you are not loving. You do not know God's Word. You are at best a fool. You are the one who needs to be sorry, who needs to be humble, and who needs to be quiet."

# 18

# ABUSER-ENABLING MISOGYNY
# IN THE CHURCH

*"To the woman he said, 'I will surely multiply your pain in childbearing; in pain you shall bring forth children. Your desire shall be for your husband, and he shall rule over you.'" (Genesis 3:16)*

*"So you will be delivered from the forbidden woman, from the adulteress with her smooth words," (Proverbs 2:16)*

*"And as if it had been a light thing for him to walk in the sins of Jeroboam the son of Nebat, he took for his wife Jezebel the daughter of Ethbaal king of the Sidonians, and went and served Baal and worshiped him."(1 Kings 16:31)*

GOD'S WORD IN HOLY SCRIPTURE is pure, right, life-giving, and true. Whenever and wherever scripture is cited to support evil, we can be sure that its real teaching has been distorted. Verses such as the ones quoted above have been very frequently twisted to misrepresent the fundamental nature of women and I want to tell you how I (and most all of you) have personally seen these distortions played out among Christians.

First, let me say very plainly that both men and women enter this world in a spiritually fallen condition – as sinners. Alienated from God. Without hope. Dead in their sins and hell-bound (see Ephesians 2). If not for the mercy of God in Christ, all would most certainly perish for all eternity. Outside of Christ, women, like men, are sinners. NOTE: Be very careful to understand that the Bible does not address real believers as sinners which they once were. The oft-repeated refrain "we are all sinners" when applied to believers is frequently a favorite tune sung by sin-levelers and sin-minimizers to enforce their demand that we forgive them and reconcile with them no matter what they have done or whether they have truly repented or not.

So yes, Eve was dead in her sins after the fall, just like Adam, as we see in Genesis three. And yes, absolutely, there are indeed "forbidden women" and "adulteresses" in this world who young men must be warned against. And certainly, there ARE Jezebels to be found, evil women who actively work to lead others into worship of their false gods. Many if not most of you have no doubt met some such woman before. (I won't take the time here to go into detail, but let's make special note that of course there are male adulterers who seduce women, who women must be warned against. And there are indeed male "Jezebels" who work to turn women away from the true and living God).

But let me describe for you how these verses and others are very commonly used to paint a picture of women in general, including Christian women, that is really nothing less that misogyny in disguise. "Misogyny" by the way, comes from the Greek verb "to hate" and the Greek noun for "women." Misogyny means "hatred of women."

Here is the **false doctrine** that is VERY often taught, overtly and covertly, in our churches by and to people who often really do desire to hold Scripture in high regard as the Word of God:

*Women, ever since the fall in Eden, are to be subservient to their husbands. In fact, women in general are subservient to men, inferior in their very nature due to the female-specific trait inherited from Eve of craving to dominate their husband, and most probably to set themselves above men in general. Women use their sexual and seductive charms to seduce and control men, and like Jezebel would lead men away from true religion in Christ.*

*These seducing and usurping traits are characteristic of Christian women as well, and the godly man who is wise must take particular care that he is not driven astray by any woman. Church leaders especially must guard against this constant, ongoing desire of women to usurp male authority in the church. Christian fathers and husbands must see to it that their wives and daughters cover themselves so that godly men are not seduced and tempted into sexual sin. Christian wives must be careful to resist their innate tendency to usurp authority over their husbands.*

Does any or all that sound familiar to you? Ironically, these doctrines are often taught by Christian women as well as Christian men.

Now, of course there is most definitely a true, wholesome, biblical teaching about modesty for all Christians. In our day (and I suppose in most every age of history) rank and wicked immodesty is characteristic of the evil world we live in. Where the Lord is rejected you always see men and women spiraling into ever-increasing degrees of sexual sin, nakedness being one such common defiance of the Law of God. But what we are speaking of in respect to this misogyny is the notion that by the very nature of the woman as woman, she tends to seduce men and lead them into sin. The extreme example of this very thinking is the teaching and practice found in some versions of Islam that require women to be essentially totally covered and hidden from view and if a woman is raped it is her fault for leading her poor rapist into the act. This strain of radical thinking regarding modesty *is also often to be found in patriarchal Christian churches and organizations.*

One young woman I know recounted to me how she was once at a youth group meeting, sponsored by her church. It was summertime and she was wearing cut-offs. She was sitting near one of the young men (who came from a very controlling, patriarchal family). The young man reached down, picked up a sweater lying nearby, and covered her legs from view. You can see the problem here. In this young man's thinking – which he had been taught on the supposed authority of Scripture – he believed that the source of the lustful thoughts he was starting to sense within himself was not his own sinful flesh, but in the young woman herself. You see the fallacy here and the damaging blame-shifting which really is misogyny. How is this young man going to view his wife one day? You can probably sort that out for yourself and the picture is not a pretty one. If he commits adultery or views porn, well, it is the fault of his wife, right? Many of you who have suffered at the hands of a domestic abuser will resonate with that claim.

So this is just a brief description of the false doctrine that I was taught about women and wives and daughters by people in the church, including many big-name Christian celebrity preachers and teachers, and I assumed for a long time that it was just a 'given' that these things must be true. After all, who was I to disagree with Bible college professors, seminary professors, Christian theologians who wrote books, and so on? I was a nobody and they, well, they were super saints with huge followings. (That is a very dangerous mentality for a Christian to have by the way and the Apostle Paul refutes it: "And from those who seemed to be influential (what they were makes no difference to me; God shows no partiality) – those, I say, who seemed influential added nothing to me." Gal. 2:6).

Now, finally, think this all through VERY carefully. Forget about parsing Greek verbs and doing intricate word studies for right now. What have YOU seen in the visible church regarding these things? I think I know the answer because I have seen the same thing. *It is NOT characteristic of a real Christian woman to constantly connive and sneak and deceive and manipulate her husband into giving her what she wants – to usurp his authority. Rather, the typical scenario we see even and especially in abuse cases is that the wife has no desire to dominate her husband, but hungers for him to be a godly man who she will willingly and gladly join hands with.* Sadly, this admirable wish on the part of the abuse victim in Christian circles is used against her to keep her in bondage to abuse. She *wants* to serve the Lord. She *wants* to be the woman and wife and mother that Christ calls her to be. And somehow the abuser diabolically senses this and turns her heart's desire against her.

There IS misogyny in the visible local church. There IS very commonly a notion, often cloaked in pious-sounding talk about the worth and value of women, mothers, and wives, that women must be kept down else before you know it men will find themselves, their churches, and their families, dominated by liberated women who are the product of devilish radical feminism that would lead us all into Baal worship. The thing is ages old, and I close with an example of it from Scripture:

*"But Queen Vashti refused to come at the king's command delivered by the eunuchs. At this the king became enraged, and his anger burned within him. Then the king said to the wise men who knew the times (for this was the king's procedure toward all who were versed in law and judgment, the men next to him being Carshena, Shethar, Admatha, Tarshish, Meres, Marsena, and Memucan, the seven princes of Persia and Media, who saw the king's face, and sat first in the kingdom): 'According to the law, what is to be done to Queen Vashti, because she has not performed the command of King Ahasuerus delivered by the eunuchs?' Then Memucan said in the presence of the king and the officials, 'Not only against the king has Queen Vashti done wrong, but also against all the officials and all the peoples who are in all the provinces of King Ahasuerus. For the queen's behavior will be made known to all women, causing them to look at their husbands with contempt, since they will say, 'King Ahasuerus commanded Queen Vashti to be brought before him, and she did not come.' This very day the noble women of Persia and Media who have heard of the queen's behavior will say the same to all the king's officials, and there will be contempt and wrath in plenty." (Esther 1:12-18)*

# 19

# Thoughts on Wolves Hiding Among the Flock

Here are excerpts from 2 Peter 2. If you can take your Bible and read the whole chapter it will help you get the "punch line" at the very end. Go for it, then I have some comments below. The boldfacing is mine:

> ***"But false prophets also arose among the people, just as there will be false teachers among you, who will secretly bring in destructive heresies,*** *even denying the Master who bought them, bringing upon themselves swift destruction. And many will follow their sensuality, and because of them the way of truth will be blasphemed. And in their greed they will exploit you with false words.* ***Their condemnation from long ago is not idle, and their destruction is not asleep....***
>
> *Bold and willful, they do not tremble as they blaspheme the glorious ones, whereas angels, though greater in might and power, do not pronounce a blasphemous judgment against them before the Lord. But these, like irrational animals, creatures of instinct,* ***born to be caught and destroyed, blaspheming about matters of which they are ignorant, will also be destroyed in their destruction,*** *suffering wrong as the wage for their wrongdoing. They count it pleasure to revel in the daytime. They are blots and blemishes, reveling in their deceptions, while they feast with you. They have eyes full of adultery, insatiable for sin. They entice unsteady souls. They have hearts*

*trained in greed. **Accursed children!** Forsaking the right way, they have gone astray....*

*These are waterless springs and mists driven by a storm. **For them the gloom of utter darkness has been reserved.** For, speaking loud boasts of folly, they entice by sensual passions of the flesh those who are barely escaping from those who live in error. They promise them freedom, but they themselves are slaves of corruption. For whatever overcomes a person, to that he is enslaved.*

***For if, after they have escaped the defilements of the world through the knowledge of our Lord and Savior Jesus Christ, they are again entangled in them and overcome, the last state has become worse for them than the first. For it would have been better for them never to have known the way of righteousness than after knowing it to turn back from the holy commandment delivered to them.*** *What the true proverb says has happened to them: "The dog returns to its own vomit, and the sow, after washing herself, returns to wallow in the mire."(2 Pet. 2:1-22)*

While there certainly are some difficult parts in this chapter, I just want to focus on two predominant themes. These relate to the question regarding whether an abuser will ever repent and change. Here are the two points drawn from this passage:

1. There are people who have come to a "knowledge" of Christ, even showing initial fruits of repentance, who return to the world and are marked out by God for eternal destruction. In other words, they are reprobate. The doors of grace are closed to them.

2. These people *can be known*. At least the kind that Peter is talking about here. He identifies them. They are false prophets. But not just any false prophet. They are people who once professed Christ. Then, like a dog returning to its vomit, they returned to their corruption.

They begin to renounce Christ by teaching heresy, denying Christ and trying to persuade others to follow them.

I suggest to you that many Christians who are abuse survivors can tell you stories about how their "Christian" spouse did this very thing. Like a pig who has been washed, he jumped back into the muck and filth of the world.

This is completely in agreement then with what we see in Hebrews 6:4-8 when we talk about people for whom repentance is now impossible.

And I want to suggest one final point which I realize will be highly controversial with many Christians. I don't write about these kinds of topics just to stir things up and get attention. Believe me, after 37 years as a pastor, the last thing I want is attention! Anyway, here is the point: I believe that the Lord does not require us to pray for such people. I think they are the kind that John had in mind when he wrote:

*"If anyone sees his brother committing a sin not leading to death, he shall ask, and God will give him life–to those who commit sins that do not lead to death. There is sin that leads to death; I do not say that one should pray for that." (1 John 5:16)*

I don't presume to have the last word on these things, and I am certainly open for everyone's comments. But please consider – do you see Peter praying for the salvation of the people he is speaking about in 2 Peter 2 (above)? Of course not. What if.....just what if....we are doing a real disservice to the work of Christ, to the world, to our churches, by failing to teach and warn that it is quite possible for a person to cross a point of no return? Does not the Bible very often caution us to not look back at Sodom, to press with violence into the kingdom of Christ, to work out our salvation with fear and trembling, and so on? Hebrews is filled with warnings like this. But our pulpits do not seem to be.

We need to be reminded that ships do not drift into safe harbor. And neither will we. Abusers sitting in our churches need to be warned clearly and plainly that if they persist in what they are doing, they will surely become the very people 2 Peter 2 is talking about. Dogs to the vomit. Pigs to the muck. We need to turn up the heat so these kind of wicked ones leave. Sin is way too comfortable in our churches. And victims of abuse are paying the price for it.

# 20

# A LETTER FROM A SILENT FOLLOWER

We are very thankful for the writer of this letter who took the time to share her experience with us. Here it is and I hope it will be a real encouragement to you as well:

THIS LETTER [edited for privacy] is so many years overdue and has gone through many revisions with me not knowing how to express myself. I feel like I know you well and you have no idea that I exist. I've prayed for you and your congregation and the many victims that have shared their stories with you. It's important that you know now that I am on the other side of it and have recovered. I am solidly in Christ.

When I was still married, I was completely convinced in my mind that suicide was the only way out of my "till death do us part" marriage vow. This was my third abusive relationship in a marriage. I was in an emotional disaster and in the "fog". It was the love of my parents that talked me off the ledge and reasoned me back to safety.

My dad was never a churchgoer because he saw them as hypocrites. My dad's family were all very outspoken evangelicals yet they did not practice what they preached to others. My dad's father was abusive to his mother, yet they all sat in church twice on Sunday. Sick. What I want to stress is that my mom and I had spent our lives in the United Methodist Church and before that the Presbyterian USA—both liberal denominations void of the true saving gospel. My mom and I had our lives revolving around church activities, mainly children's Sunday School ministries, VBS, etc... Me at my church in NC and she at her church in FL. We wore ourselves out serving with our "time, gifts, talents, and money". The UMC really uses guilt for their works-based system they call God's grace for everyone. All I ever heard about was love, grace, forgiveness and serving the community. I never heard that we were born totally depraved with nothing good in us to please God or we couldn't choose to love God on our own, never heard about evil and we never talked about sin. I believed everyone that said they were a Christian was one. It was the people outside the church that needed to come to church to have a "relationship with Jesus". That's how it was always put. Never heard language like "born again" or "conversion". So between my parents and I, none of us were saved, but had no clue. We were a "good, moral" family, but didn't know we were dead in sin.

My third abusive marriage was the turning point that changed the lives of our family for eternity. God used this evil man for good. He called himself a Christian and was well studied. My mom and dad liked him at first. He knew his theology, we could all ask him questions and he had the answers. We felt inferior to his vast knowledge. We were such fools then—completely naïve and had no discernment. We didn't have the Holy Spirit to guide and protect us, so we could not "test the spirit".

Our hard lesson came after the fog lifted and I heard the truth of the scripture you were preaching…so if my husband was a "Christian" and could be this abusive (mentally, emotionally, spiritually, psychologically, sexually, and financially) and live this evil lie every day as he did, then other people must be able to lie and wear a "Christian" mask too. I used to trust everybody and just give my trust away to anyone who was nice. I always assumed the best in people. It never crossed my mind that someone could be lying to me or have a wicked motive or malice in their heart. If someone said they were a Christian, then they were. These are all lies from the pit of Hell.

When I was searching for answers, it was only through God's mercy and grace that I even found your blog site and Sermon Audio through a Google search. By now, I think I've heard nearly every sermon at least once. I feel like I'm part of your family of followers even though I'm silent. I can't even begin to communicate the words to express my thanksgiving to you and your precious congregation for taking up this ministry to abuse victims. Through your preaching the full counsel of God, the Doctrines of Grace and the true gospel message, my parents and I have been granted saving faith in our Lord Jesus Christ. We three have been virtual members of your church for years now. We LOVE the video sermons! Now we can watch you and feel like we are there with your congregation. Thank you so much for making this technology available to us across the country. There is a little church on every corner here. We don't want anything to do with them and are so pleased to sit with our invisible remnant in the true body of Christ and share the grace and knowledge of Him. We also listen to Dr. Martyn Lloyd Jones for our Saturday morning Bible Study. I continue to live with my family and am safe. Since being saved, we have lost most all friends from the UMC church. We are very isolated here, but I'm so glad God has ordained the love and support of my parents. I do realize that is something that many abuse victims don't have.

God has arrested our attention using my evil ex-husband and it's been a sobering journey on a narrow path with much strife, battle, pain and difficulty much like Christian's journey to the Celestial City. We love our little narrow path and we love our Lord and Savior Jesus Christ! We do look forward to being together with you and your congregation in the New Creation in the Day of the Lord!

# 21

# ABUSE AS CRUELTY

*"So they ruthlessly made the people of Israel work as slaves and made their lives bitter with hard service, in mortar and brick, and in all kinds of work in the field. In all their work they ruthlessly made them work as slaves. (Exodus 1:13-14)*

*"The same day Pharaoh commanded the taskmasters of the people and their foremen, "You shall no longer give the people straw to make bricks, as in the past; let them go and gather straw for themselves. But the number of bricks that they made in the past you shall impose on them, you shall by no means reduce it, for they are idle. Therefore they cry, 'Let us go and offer sacrifice to our God.' Let heavier work be laid on the men that they may labor at it and pay no regard to lying words." (Exodus 5:6-9)*

*"Some men just want to see the world burn. They cannot be reasoned with. They cannot be appeased."*
*(Alfred to Batman about the Joker)*

ABUSERS ARE CRUEL, just as Pharaoh was cruel to the Israelites. Cruelty is a topic that deserves some serious thought because it helps us see even more clearly just how wicked the abuser is. Cruelty hurts another person (or a pet, like a puppy), but is of a particularly evil genre of hurting. Cruelty suits the mentality and character of an abuser because cruelty is exercised by someone who has power over another. Like Pharaoh's power over the enslaved Israelites, or a wicked man's boot kicking a little dog. Cruelty is the infliction of pain and suffering by a person with power, willfully and intentionally, without regard for the suffering of the victim. Cruelty (Cruella Deville and the Dalmatian puppies). And as Cruella's wicked smile demonstrates, cruelty enjoys it all.

What kind of a person enjoys cruelty? Enjoys causing a person with less power to suffer? I can tell you. A thoroughly evil person.

All of us have been guilty at one time or another of being cruel to someone. Cruelty lies within our fallen, sinful flesh looking for a chance to break out. As Christians, it is our calling and duty *and desire* to do battle against that flesh by the Spirit of Christ within us. We put cruelty to death by saying to it – "No! Go back where you came from! You will not reign over me!" When we fail in this, we are grieved and we repent. We are cut to the core in conviction when we see the tears of the person we have treated with cruelty and Christ's compassion for them breaks out in us. We hate our sin and immediately set out to make it right with the one we have so shamefully treated. We have each one been cruel, but we are not cruel people by nature.

The abuser is.

Cruelty feeds off the suffering it inflicts. Cruelty delights in the pain it causes. The abuser exults in seeing his victim suffer physical and especially emotional pain because it gives him a power rush of tyrannical domination over another. And all of this is vital for abuse victims, counselors, and pastors to understand. Why does he do that? as Lundy Bancroft puts it? Because he is evil, because he loves it, because it is who he is doing what he does. Yes, Virginia (we might say), there IS a devil!

I have been the target of numbers of such abusers over the years as they sought to work their havoc and hurt in the churches I have pastored. On and on they go – in some cases for years – creating trouble and division, launching assorted attacks, making their accusations, willfully causing pain and suffering. Why? Was it because they just weren't as sanctified as they should have been? No. Was it because I kept messing up and doing wrong to others? No. The reality was that they were just plain cruel. Cruel people who enjoyed inflicting pain and suffering in order to obtain what they just KNEW they were entitled to by nature of who they were: power and control, along with the self-glorying they so craved.

Why does an abuser prolong the child custody battle for years when his record of behavior toward the children demonstrates he cares little or nothing for them? Because he is cruel and he feeds off the pain and suffering of his victim like a drug. Why is it that he comes into the house, just looking for something to pick at, knowing full well that his victim has busted her tail that day taking care of the kids, homeschooling them, cleaning up the house, doing his laundry…. Why? Because he is cruel, and cruel people love to cause misery and pain.

This week I saw a church sign. For the most part I have grown to despise church signs. Once in a while you will see a good one but for the most part, they are statements that enable abusers. Here's the one I saw:

*"God does not force himself upon anyone, He wins their heart by love."*

Here is another one:

*"Jesus died on the cross for you so that He wouldn't have to live for eternity without you."*

These absolutely unbiblical notions are at best marvelously naive and at worst they are designed to guilt us all into seeing even the most cruel, evil person as Luke Skywalker saw Darth Vader: "Oh, Dark Lord, I just KNEW there was some good in you and that if I let you cut off my arm or even kill me, one day the good would win."

Here is the truth: Evil exists. Cruel, evil people, exist. And abusers are cruel, evil people of a particularly bad kind. No one, not even God, is going to "win their hearts by love." If you are a Christian, God did not simply love you into loving Him. He powerfully and effectually worked the truth of the gospel of Jesus Christ in you, regenerating your heart of stone and giving you a heart of flesh. He took an enemy who hated Him and transformed you by faith and repentance into His child.

These kinds of foolish platitudes (Jesus, the eternal Son of God, destined to misery if the sinner doesn't repent and come live with Him) are examples of the kind of ignorance (often willful) that abounds in the church regarding the abuser. Abusers are cruel and they are evil and they love it so. Your abuser, abuse victim, is not going to change. He has no heart to reach. He enjoys doing to you what he does because that is who he is.

And understanding that is one of the first steps to getting free.

# Appeasement of Evil is
# Impossible

*Why the western world...chose to tear itself apart in 1939 is a story not so much of accidents, miscalculations, and overreactions...as of the carefully considered decisions to ignore, appease, or collaborate with Adolf Hitler's Nazi Germany by nations that had the resources and knowledge, but not yet the willpower to do otherwise.* [2]

I CONTINUE TO SEE PARALLELS to domestic abusers (and other kinds of abusers) in our churches leap out from the pages of Hanson's excellent book. I must write about them. We can all learn and be greatly affirmed by these things because after all, evil is evil. Whether it be on a worldwide scale like the Axis powers in WWII, or hiding in our churches behind the disguise of piety.

Being neutral is by design, a choice, with results that either harm or hurt the particular parties in question – with neutrality almost always aiding the aggressive carnivore, not its victim. Or as the Indian statesman and activist V.K. Krishna Menon cynically once put it, 'there can be no more positive neutrality than there can be a vegetarian tiger.'[3]

Evil cannot be appeased. Evil lusts for power and control and will not stop until it has it, or until it is totally defeated in its attempts. Evil men consider offers of appeasement (just give him what he wants for now and he will leave us alone) not as

---

[2] The Second World Wars, by Victor Davis Hanson, Basic Books, 2017, p. 16
[3] Ibid., p. 18-19

satisfying, but as marks of weakness. Appeasement marks us as ripe targets for assault.

Think for instance of the terrible mass murders we are seeing today. Where are they occurring?

- Schools

- Churches

- Malls

- Concerts

In other words, these wicked people select their targets for the most part by zeroing in on groups of people *who are defenseless.* On people who lack the means *or the will* to shoot back, as you might put it.

Therefore, when we deal with the wicked, with abusers, with tyrants, it is a grave error and a very dangerous error, to convey the message that we either lack the means or the will to use those means to oppose an attack. And I probably don't even need to tell most of you that local churches today, pastors and members, Bible teachers and counselors, for the most part are announcing loudly and clearly that when it comes to dealing with abusers, they want to appease, to love, to be kind, to reason with, and certainly they never want to have to use the weaponry Christ has given to His church such has putting the wicked man out from among us and standing firmly with the victim. Make no mistake. Abusers can smell the scent of the kill very quickly in such an environment.

To use pre-WWII illustrations again:

The Germans sensed that the Allies had lost the power of deterrence, which is predicated not just on material strength but the appearance of it and the acknowledged willingness to use it....Almost every public proclamation that the Allies had voiced in the 1920's and early 1930's projected at least an appearance of timidity that invited war from what were still relatively weak powers....all sought international agreements...to limit arms on land and sea, to pledge peaceful intentions to one another, to showcase their virtue, to profess invincible solidarity, and even to declare war itself obsolete–anything other than to rebuild military power to shock and deter Germany.[4]

I am not trying to draw you into the realm of contemporary politics (though I hope you can see that there is timeless wisdom here for that arena), but I am attempting by way of illustration to enable all of us to see how professing Christianity has been doing really the very same thing when it comes to the evil ones who creep into the churches. Christians talk and talk and talk about "spiritual warfare." They hold conferences on the subject and write books galore about it. But in fact, in practice, most *have declared this war to be obsolete. To be beneath them. To be far too barbaric. Surely, we have become so elite and sophisticated that we must never be so ruthless as to think that evil must be met with the force of "remove such a man from among you and hand him over to Satan."* Can you hear the enemy licking his chops in such an environment?

When I lived in Alaska I always carried a firearm out in the woods. Doing so saved my wife and I from a moose attack (they are actually more dangerous in the number of attacks than grizzly bears) on the outskirts of Anchorage once. Another time we were up by Fairbanks hiking on a trail. That time I carried a short-barreled shotgun loaded with slugs and buckshot. We met some people on the trail who were going the opposite direction and there was no mistake about the look on their faces when they saw my shotgun. They looked at me in disdain and disgust. How dare I violate the sacred ground of their temple with something so barbaric as a shotgun!

And yet is this not exactly the attitude that is causing victims of abusers in our churches to continue to be oppressed and sometimes even killed? I have seen it and so have you. When I tell pastors how to confront the abuser, I am most often met with that

---

[4] Ibid

same look of disdain. How judgmental I am. How unkind. Surely I am being too harsh when I say that abusers are not to be coddled or counseled. They are to be put out from among us. I have no doubt that these kinds of pastors and "Christians" would have been quite irate at Jesus for driving the moneychanger crowd out of the temple.

Well, there are more parallels in Hanson's book that I want to share with you, but this is enough to digest for now. I close with this...well, accusation: These very kinds of denials of evil resulted in millions and millions of people being slaughtered in WWII. How many victims are suffering at the hands of the myriads of little Hitlers who hide in our churches today and who are being enabled by people with the very same foolish and sinful attitudes?

# DON'T WASTE YOUR TIME
# COUNSELING ESAU

*"Therefore let us leave the elementary doctrine of Christ and go on to maturity, not laying again a foundation of repentance from dead works and of faith toward God, and of instruction about washings, the laying on of hands, the resurrection of the dead, and eternal judgment. And this we will do if God permits. For it is impossible, in the case of those who have once been enlightened, who have tasted the heavenly gift, and have shared in the Holy Spirit, and have tasted the goodness of the word of God and the powers of the age to come, and then have fallen away, to restore them again to repentance, since they are crucifying once again the Son of God to their own harm and holding him up to contempt. For land that has drunk the rain that often falls on it, and produces a crop useful to those for whose sake it is cultivated, receives a blessing from God. But if it bears thorns and thistles, it is worthless and near to being cursed, and its end is to be burned. Though we speak in this way, yet in your case, beloved, we feel sure of better things – things that belong to salvation."(Heb. 6:1-9)*

*"For you know that afterward, when he [Esau] desired to inherit the blessing, he was rejected, for he found no chance to repent, though he sought it with tears." (Hebrews 12:17)*

IT IS MY CONVICTION that many pastors, counselors, churches and Christian ministries are wasting a lot of time. I know that in my 37 years as a pastor I have too often done the same thing. We have wasted resources, which are really the Lord's resources of which we are stewards. Time. Energy. Prayers. Money. Teaching. All for naught. The ones we were laboring to help, to save, to rescue – wouldn't have it in the end. As I look back, I can see very clearly that there were many times that I should have shaken the dust off my shoes and moved on. Increasingly this is what I do now. And so do our elders and our church members.

Notice the Scriptures above very, very carefully. Let me try to explain what I believe they mean.

When we first encounter a person who is lost in their sin, what do we do? We present them with the "elementary doctrine of Christ." We lay this foundation for them – the gospel. We call them to repentance from their dead, so-called "good works" and exhort them to turn to Christ in faith. We give them the ABC's of the New Covenant: baptism, spiritual gifts and the work of the Holy Spirit in the believer, the certain hope of the resurrection, and the promise of eternal judgment.

Now, as we do this and the person responds, they are (as Hebrews puts it) being enlightened by the Holy Spirit to the truth and reality of these things. They are "tasting" the heavenly gift and the goodness of the Word of God. They have even shared in the Holy Spirit in the sense that it is the Spirit who is showing them intimately the very "taste" of these gospel truths. The seed is sown and it has sprung up. But. . .

Some, and we could probably say "many," fall away. They go back to the world when following Christ begins to cost them something. Like a field that was blessed with abundant rain and good seed, they only bring forth a crop of thorns and thistles. The Apostle says that he hopes for better things from these professing Christians he is writing to, but nevertheless they must take care. They must see and heed the danger of becoming an Esau, for whom repentance was impossible. In Christian theology, we call these people reprobates.

Notice once again back at the beginning of the passage cited above. The Apostle is telling us – sit up and listen carefully now – he is telling us to stop doing a spiritual re-boot when dealing with people who have heard the gospel clearly, who have appeared to respond in faith and repentance, who have been enlightened by the Holy Spirit so that they know full well the gospel is true, and yet who then return to or continue in their wickedness and love for the world. Stop it, he says. You've already laid a foundation for that person. Don't go back and lay it again because you can't.

These kinds of people – people who perhaps have professed to be Christians for many years or maybe they even grew up in the church, went forward to profess Christ at an altar call, received baptism, and all the rest...these kinds of people who demonstrate by the evil fruit of their lives that they are only going to yield thorns and thistles (signs of the curse) are not to be permitted to sap our time and resources and energy. They are a waste of time. They are not going to change. They crucify Jesus Christ all over again and hold him up as it were on a cross to be mocked by the world.

Walk away! Walk away from these people. See it? The Apostle, speaking God's own Word here, is instructing us to move on and quit trying "to save" this kind.

This is why I am simply not interested in counseling abusers. Particularly abusers who use Christ as their chosen facade. Abusers who profess Jesus, who attend church, who know all their Bible verses and preach to others – abusers who have tasted the goodness of God, you see, but who only in reality bear a cursed crop of thorns. An abundant harvest of cruelty, abusive tactics, and wicked deception.

I realize that there are some Christians who do try to counsel and provide therapy for abusers. I am not trying to hammer them in any way, nor do I claim that they never do any good. But what I am saying is that when it comes to the kind of abuser that most of us here at Unholy Charade come across, God's Word tells us – don't waste your time. Give me a totally pagan man who makes no claim at all to belong to Christ. There is a man we can expend some time on laying the foundation of the gospel for him. But those who have heard, those who have tasted, those who know full well the Word of God is true – walk away. Or better, send HIM away! Your energies will be much better used being poured into the victim.

Oh, and by the way. Don't feel sorry for Esau as he sheds those crocodile tears. He isn't crying because he really wants Christ, but Christ won't have him. Nope. He is crying because he wanted the inheritance back that he squandered away for a bowl of Quaker oats. As with all abusers, his tears are selfish and have nothing to do with repentance.

# 24

# HOW COWARDICE
# ENABLES ABUSERS

*"The one who conquers will have this heritage, and I will be his God and he will be my son. But as for the cowardly, the faithless, the detestable, as for murderers, the sexually immoral, sorcerers, idolaters, and all liars, their portion will be in the lake that burns with fire and sulfur, which is the second death."(Revelation 21:7-8)*

*"No man shall be able to stand before you all the days of your life. Just as I was with Moses, so I will be with you. I will not leave you or forsake you. Be strong and courageous, for you shall cause this people to inherit the land that I swore to their fathers to give them. Only be strong and very courageous, being careful to do according to all the law that Moses my servant commanded you. Do not turn from it to the right hand or to the left, that you may have good success wherever you go." (Joshua 1:5-7)*

EVIL MUST BE NAMED. Abusers must be exposed and called to give account. Victims must be believed and protected. The cry of the oppressed must be heard. And all of this requires – courage. Why? Because those who stand with the oppressed and against the wicked will become the evil man's enemy and thus a target for his wicked tactics. Most of our readers know this full well. Just tell an abuser "no" or draw some boundary with him, and watch the fangs come out.

The enemy of courage is, of course, cowardice. As you can see from the Scriptures quoted above, the Lord does not take kindly to cowards. In fact, you cannot enter the kingdom of Christ if you are a coward. Cowards will not be found in the New Heavens and Earth. Cowards are grouped by the Lord along with the faithless, the detestable, murderers, sexually immoral, sorcerers, idolaters, and liars. The whole batch of them are headed for hell unless they repent and turn in faith to Christ. In contrast, Joshua was courageous. He courageously obeyed God's Word. He courageously led God's people against the enemy and by faith took possession of the inheritance. He was very courageous. He was a man of faith.

Lately I have seen courage and cowardice in action. Sadly, more cowardice than courage. One of the chief reasons that pastors, church leaders, church members and Christians in general quite consistently fail the abuse victim is simply and bluntly put – they are cowards. They are not willing to pay the price of standing for righteousness. Are they Christians at all? Time will tell, but apart from eventually repenting of cowardliness, well, as for the cowardly, their portion is in the lake that burns with fire. True religion, true Christianity, says James, is:

> *"Religion that is pure and undefiled before God, the Father, is this: to visit orphans and widows in their affliction, and to keep oneself unstained from the world."*
> *(James 1:27)*

Cowardliness is the fertile soil of evil. Cowards permit the wicked to take root and grow. In any human society, wicked men will inevitably come along seeking power and control for their own self-glory. Unless Christ's people courageously stand against this kind, the oppressor will take the reins of power and enslave others.

> *"I have written something to the church, but Diotrephes, who likes to put himself first, does not acknowledge our authority. So if I come, I will bring up what he is doing, talking wicked nonsense against us. And not content with that, he refuses to welcome the brothers, and also stops those who want to and puts them out of the church.*

*Beloved, do not imitate evil but imitate good. Whoever does good is from God; whoever does evil has not seen God." (3 John 1:9-11)*

"I will bring up what he is doing." There it is. John names *names*. John openly writes to the whole church – nowadays he would hit "reply all" so everyone could see it – and announce that Diotrephes is doing evil and must be called to account. Cowards don't do this. Cowards remain silent. Cowards let Diotrephes take over and lead Christ's flock astray. Many, many local churches have long ago failed to do battle when battle was necessary and the whole church now remains under the evil power of Diotrephes.

Cowardice fosters abusers and their evil. Cowardice throws victims to the wolves. Cowardice claims that Christians must always be "nice and loving" when they long ago distorted the biblical notion of love into some monstrosity Christ knows nothing of. Cowardice refuses to acknowledge the real nature of the wicked, insisting that they are just "misguided brothers in Christ." The cowardly are quite happy to sit back and let others shed blood doing battle with evil, not having to pay a price themselves, all the time quite ready to give "advice" and "criticism" to those who are actually in the frontline trenches.

Cowardice permits the wicked to flourish. It stands by when it should run to. It hesitates when action is called for. It remains silent when it is time to speak. Cowardice, you see, does not trust in Christ. Cowardice refuses to take up its cross and follow the Lord. Cowardice is evil and it allies itself with the wicked. Cowardice denies Christ, and this is what Jesus has to say about that:

*"So everyone who acknowledges me before men, I also will acknowledge before my Father who is in heaven, but whoever denies me before men, I also will deny before my Father who is in heaven." (Matthew 10:32-33)*

Cowards will not inherit the kingdom of God. A Day is coming when we will never have to see them again.

# 25

# Let's Be Patient, That's Just Who He Is

Someone who listened to one of my sermons in the *Wise as Serpents*[5] series emailed me the following:

> "My friend told me about a church she had attended where the music minister was verbally abusive. Members would "pat the hand" of the abused and apologetically say, "Don't be hurt by what he said. He's a blunt, very direct speaking person. That's just who he is.""

This comment started my memory banks of personal experience churning. And thus, this post.

Over these three decades as a pastor, I have heard that same line many times – "It's just who he/she is. Let's love him/her anyway." These kinds of people pull out the "forgiving, gracious, patient" Bible verses to support their advice. For example, when I was the new pastor at a church, the choir director was an extremely abusive person. Power, control, manipulation – that was that name of the game. The simplest suggestion would send her into a fit of anger. Uh, hello? This person is LEADING the church in the worship of God!! Do you see a problem here? Nope. Let's love her anyway.

One of the "pillars" of the church was related to her and one Sunday after the service (she had blown a cork in front of the sanctuary just before the service in front of many people) walked

---

[5] This sermon series is still posted at sermonaudio.com/crc and by the time this present book is published, we will have also published that series in book format. Wise as Serpents: Growing Wise to the Evil Among Us. Justice Keepers Publishing, available on Amazon.

up to me and said, "Now, Jeff, we all know that [insert the woman's name here] is a very bitter, angry person. But we choose to love her anyway. Let her do as she wants and there won't be any problems. It's just who she is."

And I saw it in our first church too. Same scenario – church pianist was a lady who prided herself in her stubbornness, boasting that she was the "German general." She taught a women's "Bible" study each week in her home and announced regularly that it was HER ministry and that no one in the church had anything to say about it (though a good portion of the women in her study were also members of the church). "It's just who she is, you know. But we choose to love her anyway."

And of course I could give many other stories where men were the abusive culprits that "we resolve to just love as they are."

Well, this is all bogus, totally opposed the Word of God, flat out enablement of evil, and a denial of who a true Christian really is (and is not). Try these verses on for starters:

> *"For those who live according to the flesh set their minds on the things of the flesh, but those who live according to the Spirit set their minds on the things of the Spirit. For to set the mind on the flesh is death, but to set the mind on the Spirit is life and peace. For the mind that is set on the flesh is hostile to God, for it does not submit to God's law; indeed, it cannot. Those who are in the flesh cannot please God. You, however, are not in the flesh but in the Spirit, if in fact the Spirit of God dwells in you. Anyone who does not have the Spirit of Christ does not belong to him." (Romans 8:5-9)*

> *"For if you live according to the flesh you will die, but if by the Spirit you put to death the deeds of the body, you will live. For all who are led by the Spirit of God are sons of God." (Romans 8:13-14)*

See it? God's Word says (in contradiction to what these people were saying) that who a person IS, is revealed by what that person

DOES. If a person is in fact characterized by outbursts of anger, by reviling speech toward others, by selfishness or jealousy, then that person is still living according to the flesh, their mind is hostile to God, they do not submit to God's law, nor are they able to do so even in their minds! Simply put, they are not, in any way, a Christian. A Christian is a radically changed person whose very mindset has been absolutely altered by the regenerating work of the Spirit of Christ. The sons of God are led by the Spirit of God.

So, what was the real problem of the two "worship leaders" I described above and so many others like them I have found in every church I have pastored? What was the true diagnosis? They were not saved. They were still children of wrath, dead in sin, energized by the flesh, without hope and without God in the world. Do you think that a harsh diagnosis? For myself, I find such clarity to be refreshing as it blows away all the fog of confusion such people sow among Christ's people. There it is! Mr. or Mrs. choir director. You aren't saved! Who you ARE is revealed clearly by your actions. You must repent. You must step down from leading worship. You cannot worship the God you do not know, let alone lead others in doing so.

> *"Whoever says "I know him" but does not keep his command- ments is a liar, and the truth is not in him, but whoever keeps his word, in him truly the love of God is perfected. By this we may know that we are in him: whoever says he abides in him ought to walk in the same way in which he walked." (1John 2:4-6)*

> *"Whoever says he is in the light and hates his brother is still in darkness. Whoever loves his brother abides in the light, and in him there is no cause for stumbling. But whoever hates his brother is in the darkness and walks in the darkness, and does not know where he is going, because the darkness has blinded his eyes." (1John 2:9-11)*

And on and on we could go, quoting more scriptures just like these.

What is wrong with the abuser? He is a child of the devil. For all his "God-talk" and apparent "piety" he is unsaved, unregenerate, hostile to God, an enemy of Christ's truth, and that is why he does what he does. And with this clarity in mind, what do you think now of the person who says "Oh yes, I know. He lashes out like that frequently. That's just the way he is. But he is a brother in the Lord and we need to love him anyway"? I hope that your answer is "BALONEY! THAT IS A LIE! AND THAT IS CERTAINLY NOT LOVE!"

> *"Why do you not understand what I say? It is because you cannot bear to hear my word. You are of your father the devil, and your will is to do your father's desires. He was a murderer from the beginning, and does not stand in the truth, because there is no truth in him. When he lies, he speaks out of his own character, for he is a liar and the father of lies. But because I tell the truth, you do not believe me." (John 8:43-45)*

Apparently, Jesus our Lord didn't buy it either. "Yep, that IS just the way she is. And if she doesn't repent and come to genuine faith and be saved, she is going to end in hell."

# 26

# Why Churches are Abuser-Friendly Environments

*"For certain people have crept in unnoticed who long ago were designated for this condemnation, ungodly people, who pervert the grace of our God into sensuality and deny our only Master and Lord, Jesus Christ." (Jude 1:4)*

In discussing the double life that sex offenders and other predators establish in order to gain people's trust, Anna Salter (Predators, Pedophiles, Rapists & Other Sex Offenders) quotes a man who was the youngest deacon in his church:

> "I lived a double life.... I would do kind and generous things for people. I would give families money that did not have any money that was not from the church treasury, it was from my own bank accounts. I would support them in all the ways that I could. Talk to them, encourage them. I would go to nursing homes. Talk with the elderly. Pray with the elderly. I would do community service projects. Pick up liter off the side of the road. I would mow lawns for elderly and handicapped people. Go grocery shopping for them."

But this was only his "double." The real person was actively and regularly sexually molesting children – and his children of choice were the emotionally disturbed children who no one would believe even if they told. And when two of them did tell, many people from his church came to his defense. Ultimately, he went to prison for molesting one child from the youth group he led, but in fact he had violated 95 others, all from the youth group.

As domestic abuse victims know all too well, churches are one of the most abuser-friendly environments. Even when they are reported multiple times, they are most often not prosecuted, and the victim is disbelieved. When they do go to prison, they frequently return to a church that does not know them once they are out of prison and they begin the cycle all over again. Churches usually don't bother to check the person's criminal history because the nice, "Christian" facade is so well played. Salter suggests a number of reasons why Christians are so gullible:

1.  The abuser's double life. "Niceness and likability will override a track record of molestation/abuse any day of the week."

2.  Children usually do not report being molested, especially when the perpetrator holds a position of trust in the church.

3.  Molesters realize that "church people" are easier to fool than most other people because they have a trusting mentality. They want to believe in the "good that exists in all people." [Something the Bible certainly does NOT teach, by the way!]

4.  Despite the fact that decades of research have demon-strated that people cannot reliably tell who is lying and who isn't, most people believe they can.

All of these factors also come into play in the case of domestic abusers who pose as Christians. Almost every Christian who has been victimized by an abuser will testify to this wall of refusal to believe such evil could be happening, let alone perpetrated by "such a fine Christian."

This is all intentional and dangerous naiveté. God's Word has plainly and repeatedly warned us about evil people who will come in among us. We are to test the spirits to see if they are from God. We are to expect savage wolves in sheep's clothing and examine them even if they can "baa." But we don't. We haven't been. And we are paying the piper for it. Or, more accurately, the victims are paying.

Why is being on watch and on guard considered to be mere paranoia and a lack of faith? Why are shepherds who truly watch over their flock viewed with suspicion and criticism? Why?

# 27

# FAMILY VALUES CAN
# REPLACE THE GOSPEL

*"Let no one disqualify you, insisting on asceticism and worship of angels, going on in detail about visions, puffed up without reason by his sensuous mind, and not holding fast to the Head, from whom the whole body, nourished and knit together through its joints and ligaments, grows with a growth that is from God. If with Christ you died to the elemental spirits of the world, why, as if you were still alive in the world, do you submit to regulations – 'Do not handle, Do not taste, Do not touch' (referring to things that all perish as they are used) – according to human precepts and teachings? These have indeed an appearance of wisdom in promoting self-made religion and asceticism and severity to the body, but they are of no value in stopping the indulgence of the flesh." (Col. 2:18-23)*

CHRISTIANITY IS NOT MORALISM. Moralism, in fact, is everything that Jesus Christ is not. Moralism is a system that promotes the merit of moral deeds. Of good works. Ultimately, it holds that by living a good, clean life of morality, a person will be acceptable to God. Anyone who knows anything at all about Scripture knows that this is dead set opposed to the gospel of Christ. In Christ, we are freed from slavery to sin so that we love the moral law of God and strive with a new free will to live it. Not to earn righteousness with God, but because in Christ we have that righteousness.

I would like to suggest to you that the decades of emphasis on marriage, the family, and traditional family values have taken their toll. And it isn't a good toll. "How can that be! What are you saying? That same-sex marriages, or no marriage, or abortion and so forth are good!" No, and if you have been reading this blog for very long you know that is not what we mean. But here is the problem: when morality is preached apart from the power of the gospel of Christ, it is worse than nothing. It becomes positively dangerous, and here is why –

1. As Paul wrote to the Colossians (quoted above) moral exhortations in themselves only promote a man-made, powerless religion that are NO VALUE in restraining sin. And it is even worse than that, because

2. The Law of God is the POWER of sin. Did you know that? Check it out –

*"The sting of death is sin, and the power of sin is the law."*
*(1Corinthians 15:56)*

*"Now the law came in to increase the trespass, but where sin increased, grace abounded all the more..."(Rom. 5:20)*

The Law of God is given to *excite* sin in the sinner. The problem is not with the Law, but with the sinner –

*"For while we were living in the flesh, our sinful passions, aroused by the law, were at work in our members to bear fruit for death. But now we are released from the law, having died to that which held us captive, so that we serve in the new way of the Spirit and not in the old way of the written code. What then shall we say? That the law is sin? By no means! Yet if it had not been for the law, I would not have known sin. For I would not have known what it is to covet if the law had not said, "You shall not covet." But sin, seizing an opportunity through the commandment, produced in me all kinds of covetousness. For apart from the law, sin lies dead." (Romans 7:5-8)*

Now consider this very carefully. Here we have had this avalanche of teaching: seminars, retreats, books, sermons, videos, all emphasizing marriage, the family, parenting, headship, submission.... and what has been the result? Are things significantly better in the church now than 30 years ago? Call me a pessimist, but I say that not only are they not better, they are far worse. Ask yourself this, in all of this emphasis upon marriage, the sinfulness of divorce, remarriage, the role of the husband, the role of the wife.... has Jesus Christ been emphasized and exalted? Do these books and seminars present Christ clearly? Have they pointed husbands and wives and children to Him who is the Head of the Church, apart from whom we can do nothing? I must answer, once again, in the negative.

And when you preach empty morality – empty because it looks to man alone to live it – you actually feed sin. And I suggest we have done just that. "Do this, and lie" has been our message instead of declaring –

> *"For through the law I died to the law, so that I might live to God. I have been crucified with Christ. It is no longer I who live, but Christ who lives in me. And the life I now live in the flesh I live by faith in the Son of God, who loved me and gave himself for me." (Galatians 2:19)*

Little wonder that we have an epidemic of abuse in the church.

# 28

# A Surprising Ally
## of the Abuser

*"But a man named Ananias, with his wife Sapphira, sold a piece of property, and with his wife's knowledge he kept back for himself some of the proceeds and brought only a part of it and laid it at the apostles' feet." (Acts 5:1-2)*

WE DON'T KNOW MUCH ABOUT ANANIAS. Certainly, we cannot say if he was a sociopath or the typical kind of abuser that we deal with. We do know that his sin was great and that he was a liar and hypocrite. But what I want us to consider here is his wife, Sapphira. *"with his wife's knowledge...."*.

*"And Peter said to her, 'Tell me whether you sold the land for so much.' And she said, 'Yes, for so much.' But Peter said to her, 'How is it that you have agreed together to test the Spirit of the Lord? Behold, the feet of those who have buried your husband are at the door, and they will carry you out.'" (Acts 5:8-9)*

Over the years on numerous occasions, I have had to deal with wives *who chose to take part in their husband's evil.* I think that in some of those cases the husband was an abuser, but in all these situations I am thinking of, *the wife chose to join with her wicked husband in his sin.*

Now, in addressing this subject we want to take care that we don't falsely guilt victims. I am not talking about being in the abuser's fog and being deceived for some time by him. Nor am I speaking here of a victim who for one of many understandable reasons either took a long time to leave or who perhaps has not been able to leave yet. Understood. *If you are the victim of an abuser, and if you have been unable to leave or divorce him/her, but you see the evil for what it is and you hate it and have no desire to participate in it, then you are not the kind of person I am writing about here.*

No, the people I am talking about are spouses (all women in the cases I have experienced, though this certainly could apply to a husband as well)...are spouses who *knowingly and willfully choose* the side of the wicked reviler, abuser, sociopath, etc. Like Sapphira. And then they *actively* ally with their spouse against his targets. Even though they themselves have been and probably still are subjected to their evil husband's wickedness, nevertheless they ally with him. They defend him and participate with him. For example:

- My husband is a good husband, no matter what you say.

- My husband is my hero.

- How dare you imply that about my husband?

And then there are all kinds of non-verbal ways such women ally with their evil spouse:

- They refuse to leave the marriage because of the financial or other rewards they are reaping from it.

- They cover for his religious hypocrisy and even participate in it.

- They keep his secrets.

In other words, when confronted with this:

> *"And if it is evil in your eyes to serve the LORD, choose this day whom you will serve, whether the gods your fathers served in the region beyond the River, or the gods*

*of the Amorites in whose land you dwell. But as for me and my house, we will serve the LORD." (Joshua 24:15)*

....these people choose the false god. They choose the wicked man.

One of the most typical of this kind is the pastor's wife who covers for her husband who is a wolf in wool. She knows what he is, but for personal benefit she will not expose him. In so doing, she chooses against his victims and parodies his wicked teaching and counsel to them.

These women do exist. And sometimes men are in this role as well. The ones I have known, as I said, have been women. And in the end, they fully participated in their husband's evil. They are not to be considered victims. They are Sapphiras who willfully sin with full knowledge of what their wicked husband is. The Lord knows. The Lord sees.

# 29

# MORE THOUGHTS ON THE CRUELTY
## OF THE ABUSER

*"For their rock is not as our Rock; our enemies are by themselves. For their vine comes from the vine of Sodom and from the fields of Gomorrah; their grapes are grapes of poison; their clusters are bitter; their wine is the poison of serpents and the cruel venom of asps."*
*(Deuteronomy 32:31-33)*

*"Whoever is righteous has regard for the life of his beast, but the mercy of the wicked is cruel." (Proverbs 12:10)*

CRUELTY. THINK ABOUT THAT WORD. I have written on this subject before, but it deserves further consideration. All of us at one time or another have hurt someone else, causing them some kind of pain. Before we knew Christ, perhaps we even did so intentionally. Intentionally. There it is. Cruelty is the intentional infliction of pain or suffering upon another person or an animal. The definition must continue: Cruelty is the intentional infliction of pain or suffering upon another person or animal for the mere enjoyment or satisfaction of the one inflicting it. Most of you have seen and experienced it. Comes right out of the blue. No apparent reason for the attack. Things seem fine and then BOOM! Wicked words, flying into a rage, bringing up some event from the past and making an accusation about it. WHAM! Why? Because abusers like it. They inflict pain and suffering because they enjoy doing so. Like a predator, the thirst for it builds and they must strike.

Abusers are cruel. They intentionally cause pain and suffering (physical, emotional, psychological) in their victim simply for the enjoyment of keeping them under their evil power and control. They like it. Cruelty gives them a rush. They enjoy watching the suffering. Hurt a favorite pet. Destroy a cherished possession. Threaten to injure or even kill and then watch the trauma inflicted. Abusers like it. They have much in common with those hooded medieval torture experts in the castle dungeon we see depicted in movies.

So when we are dealing with abusers we must realize that they abuse – they do all the wicked things they do, simply because they like to do it. They feed on the suffering and the sense of domination it gives them over the victim. They like it. They like it. They are cruel. Those of you who want to "reform" an abuser – did you hear me? THEY LIKE IT!

> *"Rescue me, O my God, from the hand of the wicked, from the grasp of the unjust and cruel man. For you, O Lord, are my hope, my trust, O LORD, from my youth." (Psalm 71:4-5)*

As long as a person fails to acknowledge the full weight and implications of the fact that an abuser is cruel, that he delights in inflicting suffering and trauma upon his victim to enslave and control them, such a person has no business counseling, teaching, or advising about abuse or in any abuse case.

Why does he do that? Because he is cruel. Because he feeds on the suffering of others much like his cousin the serial killer.

# 30

# THE "CHRISTIAN" ABUSER AND THE DAY OF JUDGMENT

*"When the Son of Man comes in his glory, and all the angels with him, then he will sit on his glorious throne. Before him will be gathered all the nations, and he will separate people one from another as a shepherd separates the sheep from the goats. And he will place the sheep on his right, but the goats on the left. Then the King will say to those on his right, 'Come, you who are blessed by my Father, inherit the kingdom prepared for you from the foundation of the world....*

*'Then he will say to those on his left, 'Depart from me, you cursed, into the eternal fire prepared for the devil and his angels. For I was hungry and you gave me no food, I was thirsty and you gave me no drink, I was a stranger and you did not welcome me, naked and you did not clothe me, sick and in prison and you did not visit me.' Then they also will answer, saying, 'Lord, when did we see you hungry or thirsty or a stranger or naked or sick or in prison, and did not minister to you?' Then he will answer them, saying, 'Truly, I say to you, as you did not do it to one of the least of these, you did not do it to me.' And these will go away into eternal punishment, but the righteous into eternal life." (Matthew 25:31-46)*

I HAVE STUDIED THE BIBLE'S TEACHING lately regarding this doctrine:

> *"For we must all appear before the judgment seat of Christ, so that each one may receive what is due for what he has done in the body, whether good or evil."*
> *(2 Corinthians 5:10)*

All of us, Paul says, have been issued a divine summons to appear in Christ's courtroom on that Day when He comes to judge the living and the dead. This doctrine confused me for a long time because the Bible presents it as something that the Christian should eagerly look forward to. But I didn't. Why? Because, well, how can I be excited about a Day when I have to stand before Christ and the whole universe and have not just my good works thrown up on the screen, but my sins as well? Oh yeah, I can hardly wait!

Even a Christian, and perhaps especially a Christian, is quite aware of how often we sin and how many times I have broken God's Law. I have repented. I have asked Christ's forgiveness. "If we confess our sins, He is faithful and just to forgive us our sins...." right? But then there is that Day coming in that Courtroom. Well, I now look forward to that Day. Why? Because I have come to understand that when the Bible speaks of the Day of Judgment, the judgment seat of Christ before which all will stand, it is speaking to mankind universally. To all human beings in all places and all times. Here is the fact. Every human being is going to give account. Every careless word. Every deed. But for the Christian, justified and cleansed by the blood of Christ, here is how that Day is going to go down:

> *"And he will place the sheep on his right, but the goats on the left. Then the King will say to those on his right, 'Come, you who are blessed by my Father, inherit the kingdom prepared for you from the foundation of the world. For I was hungry and you gave me food, I was thirsty and you gave me drink, I was a stranger and you welcomed me, I was naked and you clothed me, I was sick and you visited me, I was in prison and you came to me.'"*
> *(Matthew 25:33-36)*

This is why we can look forward to Christ's return and pray with gusto – "Come quickly, Lord Jesus!" It is why we are motivated to live now in a manner pleasing to Christ. I do not see any place for the notion so many of us have been taught that this Day will involve every sin of the Christian being put up on a celestial power point presentation making the believer the subject of a kind of "The Most Shocking Sins" program for all to watch.

Now, think this through carefully. If an abuser can be an abuser, if he can be a person with a profound sense of entitlement (me, myself, I, center of the universe) to possess power and control over others, and who possesses a sense of conscienceless justification in using whatever tactics are necessary to possess that control and enforce it, AND be a real Christian who has been born again, forgiven, justified in Christ, indwelt by the Spirit of God (yet somehow sanctification just never took off in him, hmmm??) then your abuser, every "Christian" abuser who has so wickedly oppressed all of you, IS GOING TO SKATE ON THAT DAY. Because remember, "there is therefore now no condemnation for them that are in Christ Jesus." "Therefore, having been justified by faith we have peace with God." Right? Am I right? Yes, because God's Word is right.

The wicked WILL skate on that Day IF a person can be wicked, their very nature defined by evil, habitually walk in sin without anything but the typical fake "repentance," AND be a Christian.

But it isn't going to happen. The wicked will not escape the justice of Christ on that Day. Their teeth will be smashed. Their houses will be a desolation. They will hear the Judge send them away into outer darkness where there will be weeping and wailing and gnashing of teeth. No man can mock God. No one can claim the name of Jesus Christ and yet habitually and without repentance walk in sin.

Here is proof. Read and be encouraged. Justice, perfect justice is coming. And not a word of condemnation for those who truly are in Christ Jesus! Come Lord Jesus! Come and make it all right!

> *"For those who live according to the flesh set their minds on the things of the flesh, but those who live according to the Spirit set their minds on the things of the Spirit. For to set the mind on the flesh is death, but to set the mind on the Spirit is life and peace. For the mind that is set on the flesh is hostile to God, for it does not submit to God's law; indeed, it cannot. Those who are in the flesh cannot please God. You, however, are not in the flesh but in the Spirit, if in fact the Spirit of God dwells in you. Anyone who does not have the Spirit of Christ does not belong to him." (Romans 8:5-9)*

> *"So then, brothers, we are debtors, not to the flesh, to live according to the flesh. For if you live according to the flesh you will die, but if by the Spirit you put to death the deeds of the body, you will live." (Romans 8:12-13)*

> *"And by this we know that we have come to know him, if we keep his commandments. Whoever says "I know him" but does not keep his commandments is a liar, and the truth is not in him, but whoever keeps his word, in him truly the love of God is perfected. By this we may know that we are in him: whoever says he abides in him ought to walk in the same way in which he walked.*

> *Beloved, I am writing you no new commandment, but an old commandment that you had from the beginning. The old commandment is the word that you have heard. At the same time, it is a new commandment that I am writing to you, which is true in him and in you, because the darkness is passing away and the true light is already shining. Whoever says he is in the light and hates his brother is still in darkness. Whoever loves his brother abides in the light, and in him there is no cause for stumbling. But whoever hates his brother is in the darkness and walks in the*

*darkness, and does not know where he is going, because the darkness has blinded his eyes." (1 John 2:3-11)*

*"Now concerning brotherly love you have no need for anyone to write to you, for you yourselves have been taught by God to love one another," (1 Thessalonians 4:9)*

*"We love because he first loved us. If anyone says, 'I love God,' and hates his brother, he is a liar; for he who does not love his brother whom he has seen cannot love God whom he has not seen. And this commandment we have from him: whoever loves God must also love his brother." (1 John 4:19-21)*

*"So, every healthy tree bears good fruit, but the diseased tree bears bad fruit. A healthy tree cannot bear bad fruit, nor can a diseased tree bear good fruit. Every tree that does not bear good fruit is cut down and thrown into the fire. Thus you will recognize them by their fruits. "Not everyone who says to me, 'Lord, Lord,' will enter the kingdom of heaven, but the one who does the will of my Father who is in heaven." (Matthew 7:17-21)*

# 31

# Spiritual Sounding Talk
# Oppresses the Innocent

I WAS READING THE COMMENTS today on a Facebook page of an abuse survivor. She posted some excellent material challenging the church to wake up to domestic abuse in its midst. Then this fellow Michael came along and here is what he said:

> "There is an all-out assault by Satan and his angels upon husbands, wives, and their children in America today. We must rise up in prayer to wage war against it. Realizing we are in a spiritual war against principalities and powers of darkness, and, we wrestle not against flesh and blood. Read the book of Ephesians chapter 6 verses 10-18. Get the full armor on! Sometimes our greatest weapons against the Devil's attacks are unconditional love, forgiveness from the heart, & honest intercessory prayers for our perceived enemies. Blessing those who curse us with painful abusive treatment. God is mighty to save all those who practice His principles of war."

How holy these words sound. How pious. How biblical. How wise. Wrong! And I am going to show you why. I suppose we should do what Michael recommends and read the Scripture –

> *"Finally, be strong in the Lord and in the strength of his might. Put on the whole armor of God, that you may be able to stand against the schemes of the devil. For we do not wrestle against flesh and blood, but against the rulers, against the authorities, against the cosmic powers over this present darkness, against the spiritual forces of evil in the heavenly places. Therefore take up the whole armor of*

*God, that you may be able to withstand in the evil day, and having done all, to stand firm.*

*Stand therefore, having fastened on the belt of truth, and having put on the breastplate of righteousness, and, as shoes for your feet, having put on the readiness given by the gospel of peace. In all circumstances take up the shield of faith, with which you can extinguish all the flaming darts of the evil one; and take the helmet of salvation, and the sword of the Spirit, which is the word of God, praying at all times in the Spirit, with all prayer and supplication. To that end keep alert with all perseverance, making supplication for all the saints…" (Ephesians 6:10-18)*

When people like Michael make comments like he did (quoted above) the real harm that is done is in what is NOT said. Michael's advice would inevitably communicate to the victim of an abuser that her response to the abuse is to be passive. Armor up, then keep letting the darts come. Notice also that he starts off with the not-so-vague premise that what the victim and all of us must do is preserve the marriage and family as the primary goal. That's the real problem, says Michael. And therefore, he continues, we must all "rise up in prayer." What does that mean? I can tell you what the abuse victim who earnestly desires to seek the Lord's will in her life will take it to mean – she is to do nothing but pray.

And then Michael unleashes his big guns that do even more devastating damage. Unconditional love. Forgiveness from the heart (no mention of repentance by the abuser here). Honest intercessory prayer for our perceived enemies – and what are we meant to infer from that word 'perceived'? It is clear that Michael would think it wrong to perceive an abuser as an enemy. Is there any doubt that Michael is saying: "Hey everyone, you need to get that log out of your eye and stop perceiving that individual as an enemy. A covenant-breaking spouse needs to be cut some slack by his victim and the rest of us because, after all, "the devil made him do it. ... Bless your abuser, victim, and stand back and watch God save his soul."

This stuff is just plain spew. Oh, how wonderful and biblical it sounds. But it is wicked. It is enslaving.

Take another look at the Ephesians passage and as you do, watch carefully for the ACTIVE words. Specifically, notice how often TRUTH is involved in the armor. You see, people like Michael, if pinned down, cannot really even tell you precisely WHAT the armor of the Lord is. *"Read Ephesians 6. Put on the armor. Armor up. Stand."* But what does that mean, Michael? Tell us. What is each article of the armor and specifically how is it to be USED? The passivity that Michael foists upon the abuse victim guts this Scripture of the active weaponry to be launched against evil. Yes, pray. But pray for what? Just the salvation of the abuser? What about prayer as in the Psalms? Prayers that ask the Lord to kill the wicked and obliterate their memory from the face of the earth? And Ephesians tells us to extinguish all the flaming darts of the evil one. These are the lies and distortions which abusers (the devil's agents) love to spread. Yes, we must stand. But for what? What about TRUTH – the truth of the Word of God that exposes for all to see the evil tactics being done in darkness by the abuser? That seems to have slipped Michael's mind.

You blew it Michael. Will you admit it? I doubt it. I wish you would, but I'm not holding my breath. For all the rest of you, breathe easy and realize that Michael's advice is bogus.

# 32

# How to Put on Christ When You Are Accused

*"For freedom Christ has set us free; stand firm therefore, and do not submit again to a yoke of slavery." (Gal. 5:1)*

ALL CHRISTIANS and in some ways in particular, those who have been victims of crafty abusers who parade as most eminent and holy Christians, have been the target of false accusations and condemnation, all designed to lead us to despair of having forgiveness of sins in Christ. This is a common tactic of the enemy and we must be wise to it. Listen to these words by Martin Luther as he comments on Paul's Epistle to the Galatians:

"Let us bear this in mind when the devil accuses and frightens our conscience, attempting to drive us to despair. He is the father of lying and the enemy of Christian freedom; he torments us every moment with false fears, so that when our conscience has lost this Christian freedom, it will feel remorse for sin and condemnation and always remain in anguish and terror. When that great dragon– that old snake, the devil– comes and tells you that not only have you done no good, but you have also transgressed God's law, say to him, 'You are troubling me with the memory of my past sins; you are also reminding me that I have done no good. But this is nothing to me, for if I either trusted in my own good deeds or feared because I have done no such deeds, Christ would in either case be of no value to me at all. I rest only in the freedom Christ has given me. I know he is of value to me, and so I will not make him of no value, which I would be doing if I either presumed to purchase favor and everlasting life for myself by my good deeds or despaired of my salvation because of my sins.'

Let us learn, then, carefully to separate Christ from all that we do, both good and evil, from all laws, both human and divine, and from all troubled consciences. Christ has nothing to do with any of these. He does have something to do with afflicted consciences but not to afflict them further, but to raise them up and in their affliction comfort them. If Christ seems like an angry judge or a lawgiver who requires a strict account of our past life, then let us assure ourselves that is not Christ, but a raging fiend. The Scripture depicts Christ as our reconciliation, our advocate, and our comforter. He is and always will be such; he cannot be unlike himself.

The devil will disguise himself in the likeness of Christ and argue with us as follows: 'You were admonished by my Word and ought to have done this, but you have not done it; you ought not to have done that, and you have done it; be sure that I will take vengeance on you.' When he does this, we should not let it move us at all but should immediately think, 'Christ does not speak like this to poor, afflicted, and despairing consciences. He does not add affliction to the afflicted; he does not break the 'bruised reed' or snuff out the 'smoldering wick' (Isaiah 42:3). It is true that he speaks sharply to the hard-hearted, but if people are afraid and afflicted, he entices them most lovingly and comfortingly (Matt. 9:2, 13; 11:28; Luke 19:10; John 16:33). We must take good care, therefore, that we are not deceived by Satan's tricks and receive an accuser and condemner instead of a comforter and Savior.[6]

Pretty good stuff, right? Christian, Christ is your Friend, not your accuser!

---

[6] Martin Luther, Galatians; *The Crossway Classic Commentaries*

# 33

# Ministry to Abuse Victims Is True Prison Ministry

*"Remember those who are in prison, as though in prison with them, and those who are mistreated, since you also are in the body." Hebrews 13:3*

PRISON AND JAIL ministries are common among Christians. And they can be a very good thing. Prisoners have found Christ in their confinement.

But the prison ministry spoken of in Scripture is different. It isn't really a ministry to the likes of the two thieves beside Jesus. When the Bible speaks of prison ministry, it is talking about ministry to Christians who have been locked up for their profession of Christ. And so you have –

*"I, Paul, write this greeting with my own hand. Remember my chains. Grace be with you. (Colossians 4:18)*

*"I was naked and you clothed me, I was sick and you visited me, I was in prison and you came to me." (Matt. 25:36)*

*"For you had compassion on those in prison, and you joyfully accepted the plundering of your property, since you knew that you yourselves had a better possession and an abiding one." (Hebrews 10:34)*

Today, while there might be an occasional prisoner in this country who is in prison for his profession of Christ, it just isn't common (though in other parts of the world it is very real). What is common here, however, is the prison of abuse. Abuse victims are in prison. They will tell you so. Just listen to their stories. Isolation. Shame. Economic deprivation. Their warden is their abuser. Abuse is a prison. There is no freedom. Their every move- ment is often monitored and controlled.

So, when we minister to abuse victims, we are fulfilling our Lord's command that we remember those who are in prison. And we do it with a spirit of being in that prison with them. We are all one body. One part suffers, everyone suffers.

And therefore, it is well past time for churches to start real, biblical prison ministries. And here is a really great thing about this kind of jail ministry – we can actually spring the prisoner out and set them free.

# 34

# YOUR CHURCH NEEDS TO STINK

ONE OF THE MOST COMMON SCENARIOS that Christian domestic abuse victims relate to me is that after they have asked their church for help with the abuser, they have not been believed. Then, after a characteristic progression of events, the victim determines that she must separate from and/or divorce her abuser. At this point a great injustice is done. The victim is labeled as the culprit because she is perceived as the one who ended the marriage. The abuser, successful in his work of gaining allies, is perceived by many people as being the *victim*. The abuser, in the end, remains in the church while the victim must depart. We are not exaggerating this claim, and many victims will testify to this.

We *should* see people leaving our churches. But we must take care that it is the guilty and not the innocent who are departing! If you know much at all about the mentality and tactics of abuse then you know that abusers very typically exhibit Jekyll/Hyde behavior. They wear a mask. They put on a façade. And when they choose the façade of Christianity, they are particularly deceiving and dangerous. Therefore, a healthy, true church will be a place where this masquerade is exposed, where darkness has Christ's Light shined upon it, and in which ultimately the abuser will no longer be able to hide. He must repent, or he must flee.

> *"They went out from us, but they were not of us; for if they had been of us, they would have continued with us. But they went out, that it might become plain that they all are not of us." (1 John 2:19)*

*"I am the true vine, and my Father is the vinedresser. Every branch in me that does not bear fruit he takes away, and every branch that does bear fruit he prunes, that it may bear more fruit." (John 15:1-2)*

Do you ever see people leaving your church? We have experienced this many times over the years, and often when it happens, other people can be thrown into confusion. "Why did so and so leave?" The assumption is that someone has done something wrong, offended them, or something of that nature. And I suppose that charge is true. We have done something to offend them – we have proclaimed and lived out the gospel of Christ. The cross is an offense. Darkness hates the light because the deeds of darkness are evil. Christ's people are a stench of death to those who are perishing –

*"For we are the aroma of Christ to God among those who are being saved and among those who are perishing, to one a fragrance from death to death, to the other a fragrance from life to life. Who is sufficient for these things? For we are not, like so many, peddlers of God's word, but as men of sincerity, as commissioned by God, in the sight of God we speak in Christ." (2 Cor. 2:15-17)*

The town I live in stinks! It is a cow town. I grew up around cows, but even for me the smell around here gets really rank when the farmers spread manure on their fields that has "cooked" in storage for a long time. The old-timers say "ahhh, that's the smell of money!" (thinking of the grass this rotten stuff will grow!). That's how it must be when an abuser in disguise comes to our churches. A healthy, genuine church, in other words, will *stink* to the abuser. Try as he might, he must plug his spiritual nose and eventually depart. He can only fake it for so long.

So, we ask you – does your church *stink to evil men*? Is it a life-giving aroma to victims? Or is it the other way around?

# 35

# WHO IS RESPONSIBLE TO "FIX" A MARRIAGE COVENANT?

WHY IS IT THAT when he is wrong, I am the one who always feels guilty?

That's a pretty good question, isn't it? I heard that in a movie once. It was made by the sister of a sociopathic family member who kept everyone else in chaos and confusion by her selfish antics and blaming. The movie was a comedy. Real life isn't.

This morning I came across a couple of very, very common statements that we find in books and articles and sermons about marriage and divorce. And it struck me – these statements are actually putting the burden of responsibility for preserving the marriage onto the INNOCENT party! Here they are. See what you think – (find them on page 2546 of the ESV Study Bible),

> "In the case of adultery, divorce is allowed but not required. In fact, forgiveness and reconciliation, restoring the marriage, should always be the first option."

And again –

> "But it must be emphasized that, if reconciliation of the marriage can at all be brought about, that should always be the first goal."

We hear this stuff all the time, right? Now, I want to make some observations here:

1. Isn't the FIRST option/goal in cases where the marriage covenant has been violated, REPENTANCE on the part of the offender?

2. When we say that forgiveness and reconciliation are the first goal (slap me to my senses here if I am wrong), are we not bypassing the guilty party and running right to the victim and saying "OK, now it is YOUR duty to fix this marriage. YOU must forgive and reconcile"?

Is it not more in keeping with the nature of marriage as a covenant to say: "This marriage covenant has been destroyed by adultery/abuse. Mrs. Victim, you have the right to divorce. Mr. Perpetrator, Christ calls you to repent. But even if you do repent, she does not have to remain married to you. She will forgive you. But it is her legal, covenantal right to divorce you."

Is it really true that restoring the marriage should always be the first option? Abuse victims who have sorted it out will answer, "No way!" In fact, that is probably the worst thing to do.

Think about it. When we talk about forgiveness and reconciliation, whom are we addressing? The VICTIM, obviously. The abuser isn't going to be forgiving anyone – though he will try hard to make you think he is really the wronged party. And he sure isn't going to be the one working to reconcile the marriage. He has been doing just the opposite and he will continue to do so.

What is the first priority in cases of abuse, or other situations where the marriage covenant has been destroyed by horrendous sin that smashes the vows? The first priority is to tell the victim what her rights are. A civil judge would do that. An attorney would do that. But the church? Well, we don't seem to be doing this. We lay the load on the poor victim. And that is just wrong.

# 36

# WHY WON'T THEY BELIEVE ME?

WHY IS IT THAT if a man goes to church, people find it hard to believe that he can abuse his wife mentally or physically? I would have to answer this question in two parts:

1.  He is a master of disguise, and

2.  Christians often fail to take seriously the many warnings of Scripture.

We naïvely think that because WE think or act in a particular manner, then that is how everyone else must think and act too. We profess to be Christians. We go to church. We pray. We read our Bibles. And we do so because we sincerely desire to follow Christ. Therefore, surely – we think – everyone else who does these things must be a genuine Christian too. But we are quite mistaken, and we really should know better in light of the plain and repeated warnings Christ gives us in His Word. For example:

> *"Beware of false prophets, who come to you in sheep's clothing but inwardly are ravenous wolves." (Matt. 7:15)*

> *"But false prophets also arose among the people, just as there will be false teachers among you, who will secretly bring in destructive heresies, even denying the Master who bought them, bringing upon themselves swift destruction. And many will follow their sensuality, and because of them the way of truth will be blasphemed." (2 Peter 2:1-2)*

> *"But I am afraid that as the serpent deceived Eve by his cunning, your thoughts will be led astray from a sincere*

*and pure devotion to Christ. For if someone comes and proclaims another Jesus than the one we proclaimed, or if you receive a different spirit from the one you received, or if you accept a different gospel from the one you accepted, you put up with it readily enough." (2 Cor. 11:3-4)*

*"For such men are false apostles, deceitful workmen, disguising themselves as apostles of Christ. And no wonder, for even Satan disguises himself as an angel of light. So it is no surprise if his servants, also, disguise themselves as servants of righteousness. Their end will correspond to their deeds." (2 Cor. 11:13-15)*

Need I cite more? So why then do we find it so shocking that a person can come into our churches, speak like a Christian, pray like a Christian, behave like a Christian – yet be a devil in disguise? I can only say that we are careless and/or we do not believe God's Word. We think too highly of ourselves and others. We are ignorant of the nature and depth of sin because we do not apply ourselves diligently to the study of God's Word. So, we are flabbergasted – no, we don't even get that far. We are not shocked that the abuser is doing the evil his victim reports. We simply don't believe her, because in our minds, such a thing just cannot or could not be. It *just can't be*! We are ignorant of the thing. Unlike the Puritans, we don't write books today like The Sinfulness of Sin.

In addition, perhaps *we just don't want to pay the price that standing against an abuser will cost us*. To believe the victim means that her abuser is NOT what we have assumed he was. He may have duped us into letting him become a leading church member, serving on committees, being an important donor, etc. We must admit that we have been fooled. That is humbling. But we should not be so ashamed – we need not think so highly of ourselves. The fact is that wicked people are very, very good at disguising themselves. A demon can come as an angel of light! That's a pretty good disguise! Eventually, however, if the church is a true church, the Spirit of Christ by the Word of Christ will expose him for what he or she is. If he repents, this will be the result:

*"But if all prophesy, and an unbeliever or outsider enters, he is convicted by all, he is called to account by all, the secrets of his heart are disclosed, and so, falling on his face, he will worship God and declare that God is really among you." (1Cor. 14:24-25)*

If he refuses to repent, he will leave because he will simply not be able to stand the Light.

Here is still another reason that I believe is more common than we might realize. Many times professing Christians and professing Christian churches are *not Christ's at all*. And I am afraid that there is far more of this very scenario today than most would suspect. The Levite and the Priest bypassed the man who had been beaten and robbed. Why? They were quite religious, but they were whitewashed tombs, rotten on the inside. The "church" at Laodicea was almost no church at all yet it looked to be quite successful. I absolutely cannot imagine that the people who covered up Christa Brown's abuse, covering for the pastor who molested her, could have been genuinely, regenerate, true Christians indwelt by the Spirit of Christ (See her book, *This Little Light*).

Finally (there may well be more reasons too), pastors and Christians may not believe the victim because they have been caught up in the many unbiblical traditional teachings about marriage, divorce, headship and submission. Unaware of the real nature of the mentality and tactics of the abuser, Christians counsel the victim to do better at submitting, to try harder to not trigger her husband's (or wife's) hot buttons, and do everything that can be done to preserve the marriage. Thus, this kind of thinking goes, the abuser can be won to Christ. He or she is simply an unsaved person, and by patiently enduring and suffering, the victim can be used to bring them to repentance and faith in Christ. Of course, this is not the proper manner to deal with the abusive mentality, who is very often a sociopath, lacking any conscience. For these reasons and more, the victim is frequently sent back to her terror.

# 37

# WE NEED TO STOP TELLING ABUSE VICTIMS WHAT TO DO

*"Who are you to pass judgment on the servant of another? It is before his own master that he stands or falls. And he will be upheld, for the Lord is able to make him stand. One person esteems one day as better than another, while another esteems all days alike. Each one should be fully convinced in his own mind." (Romans 14:4-5)*

WHEN A VICTIM OF ABUSE comes to us, it is very easy for us to launch into a "fix-it" mode and start telling her what she should do.  We need to stop doing this, and for several reasons:

- She has been told what to think and what to do by her abuser, probably for a long time. Now it is time that she is allowed to think on her own.

- We inevitably view her situation far too simplistically when we respond with "shoulds."

- We really don't know what is best for her in her particular situation.

Of course, this does not mean that we don't tell her anything. There are basics, depending upon where she is at in her realization of what is happening to her, that we can and should tell her such as what the signs are of a life-threatening situation. But providing her with information is far different than telling her what she should or should not do.

You probably already know that Christians and pastors and churches readily start dumping what we are convinced is God's Word to her. Divorce is never permitted. You need to submit to him. You should forgive him if he is sorry. And on and on. In fact, what we need to do is (assuming we really know what we are talking about, which few of us really do) provide her with information, help, safety, and so on.

In my opinion (and I am pretty sure I'm right!) we tell people what they must do far too often. Understand, I am not promoting some kind of "sin as much as you want" and we will never, never admonish you scenario. Of course not. What I am concerned with however are issues of life that really are matters of one's conscience. We regularly elevate such matters into the category of sin/not sin. Right or wrong. Holy or unholy.

The issue of divorce and remarriage is an example. Really, what right do we as Christians or pastors have to dictate to a victim of abuse whether or not she can divorce her abuser? Unless we actually believe (and unfortunately, some do) that divorce is NEVER permitted for abuse, then what in the world are we doing dictating to her what to do? The truth is, she has the right to decide. Our job is to provide her with information and counsel about abuse, about abusers, about what is really happening to her and what its effects are on her and her children. But she is the one, in the end, who must decide to stay or divorce, and she is the one who has to live with her decision. Each one should be fully convinced in his own mind. That is God's word on the matter.

# 38

## ABUSE AND GENDER - WHEN
## BROTHERHOOD GOES WRONG

*"I commend to you our sister Phoebe, a servant of the church at Cenchreae, that you may welcome her in the Lord in a way worthy of the saints, and help her in whatever she may need from you, for she has been a patron of many and of myself as well. Greet Prisca and Aquila, my fellow workers in Christ Jesus, who risked their necks for my life, to whom not only I give thanks but all the churches of the Gentiles give thanks as well. Greet also the church in their house. Greet my beloved Epaenetus, who was the first convert to Christ in Asia. Greet Mary, who has worked hard for you." (Rom. 16:1-6)*

THERE IS A PLACE for male brotherhood. When men band together into a "band of brothers" for a righteous cause, it is a wonderful thing. You see it in times of war. You have it in Scripture in the example of David's "mighty men" who displayed the virtue of intense self-denial and loyalty:

*"And David said longingly, 'Oh, that someone would give me water to drink from the well of Bethlehem that is by the gate!' Then the three mighty men broke through the camp of the Philistines and drew water out of the well of Bethlehem that was by the gate and carried and brought it to David. But he would not drink of it. He poured it out to the LORD and said, 'Far be it from me, O LORD, that I should do this. Shall I drink the blood of the men who went*

*at the risk of their lives?' Therefore he would not drink it.*
*These things the three mighty men did." (2 Sam. 23:15-17)*

So, a band of brothers is a great thing as long as the team's goals are those of the Lord's. Bands of godly brothers will be one of the greatest resources of protection for the weak, innocent, and abused. But alas, the band can so easily turn into a gang.

As we have mentioned before at *Unholy Charade*, the experiences of Christian women when they report abuse to their church leaders is very often not a story of virtue and noble, valiant protection being afforded her. Rather, the sad state of affairs so frequently turns out to be brotherhood gone wrong. Men with power in a church abuse that power, cling together, and oppress the victim. And it seems to me that this is very often done without the church leaders really seeing their prejudice operating. There is a blindness to the thing. And yet it is there. It needs to be exposed, admitted, and talked about.

"Birds of a feather flock together," as the old saying goes. Races, genders, nationalities, occupational groups – they gravitate together just as the language groups did after Babel. But these bands can go bad. Honda Goldwing owners can find themselves spurned by Harley-Davidson riders. Chevy vs. Ford. And then it gets uglier. White against black. Black against white. Men against women. Women against men. The school of fish in which we swim becomes the definition of right to power and control.

The Christian brotherhood is a wonderful band, but when it turns into a gang, well, many of our readers will be able to testify of the terrible and painful results. Men, without perhaps realizing it, stick together simply because they are men. When a woman comes along, telling her story of abuse at the hands of one of their brothers, there is a serious choice to make. Often it is not the right one. We are men. She is a woman. In the church, we hold power and control and it must be maintained. We don't call it power and control. We call it pastoring, or shepherding, or headship. But quite often – perhaps even most often – it really comes down to "us against them."

Which brings us back to Romans 16, quoted above. Go through the list. The Apostle Paul names both men and women in his warm greetings and commendations. We often skip right over these lists – there are others in the New Testament. But I think that one important lesson we can take from them is that there is no hint in them of a male gang. Women are regarded as fellow-heirs and fellow laborers in Christ. I am not addressing here the whole matter of the roles of men and women in the church. I am simply saying that the Scripture does not teach us that men are superior to women, that men are in some exclusive brotherhood from which women are banned. Quite the contrary.

And therefore, I challenge every local church, every Christian pastor, church leader, church member, husband, and man to take a long, honest look at how we think about men and about women. The day that a woman in our church comes to us for help and protection from abuse will be the day that our real thoughts on these matters will be exposed. So far, and for the most part, what we are seeing is an indecent exposure of which all Christians should be ashamed.

# 39

# TAKING RESPONSIBILITY TO HELP
## ABUSE VICTIMS

*Then the LORD said to Cain, "Where is Abel your brother?"*
*He said, "I do not know; am I my brother's keeper?"*
*(Genesis 4:9)*

IT IS OUR JOB, given to us by Christ, to protect the defenseless. The civil authorities are appointed by Christ to strike fear into the evildoer (Romans 13), but there is another institution appointed by Christ that also bears the responsibility and that is the Church. Us. Christians. If we are to obey Christ, then we must acknowledge and shoulder this responsibility. But in many cases, we are not doing so. In previous articles, we exposed the many devices used by churches, pastors and individual Christians to "pass the buck." Ultimately, we cannot pass it. The job of defending and protecting the defenseless is given to us, and the buck stops here.

In his history of the Second World War, Volume I, Winston Churchill documents how denial, a dangerous naiveté about "peace in our time," and other foolish ideas resulted in the near destruction of Britain at the hands of Hitler. There were years and years before the war when many warnings were given that Germany was re-arming in violation of the Treaty of Versailles. Buck was passed. Black and white was denied. No action was taken. And eventually the slaughter began. Churchill said that in those years, he was reminded of some lines he read in a cartoon book when he was only a child. And this is how they read –

*Who is in charge of the clattering train?*
*The axles creak and the couplings strain,*
*And the pace is hot, and the points are near,*
*And Sleep has deadened the driver's ear;*
*And the signals flash through the night in vain,*
*For Death is in charge of the clattering train.*

That is what the evil of abuse is like so often in the setting of the church. It is a train running out of control, or rather, under the control of Death. The signals are flashing their warnings – but to no avail. The rest of the church sleeps. And the train rumbles on until…it is too late.

It is our job – the job of every single Christian and every single local church – to take back the train controls. A local church, united in support of an abuse victim, knowledgeable of the evil mentality and tactics of this wicked sin called abuse, is a powerful and really unstoppable force against evil. We can give the victim the means to get free. We can provide her with necessities – food, clothing, shelter, protection. We can vindicate her by rejecting her abuser's accusations. We can refuse to permit the abuser to continue to practice his hypocrisy in our church. We can do all of this and so much more. The Christian church has the potential to be the greatest single institution on earth to aid and rescue victims of abuse–far greater than the civil authorities all combined.

If you are a genuine Christian and not one in name only, the time comes when you simply cannot continue to sleep the sleep of denial. We must wake up, hear the warning signals, and wrest control of the train back from Death.

# 40

# Abusive Tactics -
# the Kiss of Judas

*"While he was still speaking, there came a crowd, and the man called Judas, one of the twelve, was leading them. He drew near to Jesus to kiss him, but Jesus said to him, "Judas, would you betray the Son of Man with a kiss?"*
*(Luke 22:47-48)*

IT IS THE NATURE OF SIN to deceive and to destroy. Satan is the father of lies and he was a murderer from the beginning. He deceives in order to destroy. These elements are really present in the heart of any sin, but we see them very clearly illustrated in the nature, mentality, and tactics of the abuser. This is why I maintain that any pastor or any Christian who desires to know the nature of sin, how we can expect it to operate, and how it thinks, can do nothing better than to study domestic violence and abuse in depth.

This will resonate with abuse victims. The kiss of Judas. They have received it. Their abuser, claiming to love them and have their welfare at heart, professing to be a servant of Christ, kisses with his lips while holding a concealed dagger in his hand. Christians of all people should be aware of this, as Scripture plainly tells us these things. But Judas was good at his craft and so are his offspring. Jesus was never deceived by him of course, but the rest of the disciples were, and they were in rather intimate contact with him for 2-3 years.

*"Mary therefore took a pound of expensive ointment made from pure nard, and anointed the feet of Jesus and wiped his feet with her hair. The house was filled with the*

*fragrance of the perfume. But Judas Iscariot, one of his disciples (he who was about to betray him), said, 'Why was this ointment not sold for three hundred denarii and given to the poor?' He said this, not because he cared about the poor, but because he was a thief, and having charge of the moneybag he used to help himself to what was put into it." (John 12:3-6)*

I don't know if anyone knows if Judas was married or not but imagine being his wife! Ah, an eminent apostle of Christ! Poor lady!

In the end, Judas went out and hanged himself. And so it will be for all wicked, deceitful, abusive human beings who persist in their evil and refuse to repent. That great Day is coming when everything is going to be brought to light and when much that is being done in Jesus' name today will be found out to be wood, hay, and stubble. The chaff will not stand in the judgment, nor sinners in the assembly of the righteous (Psalm 1). Such Judas' can kiss all they want. It will do them no good.

# 41

# CONFRONTING ABUSE - BE LIKE JOHN THE BAPTIST

*"At that time Herod the tetrarch heard about the fame of Jesus, and he said to his servants, 'This is John the Baptist. He has been raised from the dead; that is why these miraculous powers are at work in him.' For Herod had seized John and bound him and put him in prison for the sake of Herodias, his brother Philip's wife, because John had been saying to him, 'It is not lawful for you to have her.' And though he wanted to put him to death, he feared the people, because they held him to be a prophet.*

*But when Herod's birthday came, the daughter of Herodias danced before the company and pleased Herod, so that he promised with an oath to give her whatever she might ask. Prompted by her mother, she said, 'Give me the head of John the Baptist here on a platter.' And the king was sorry, but because of his oaths and his guests he commanded it to be given. He sent and had John beheaded in the prison, and his head was brought on a platter and given to the girl, and she brought it to her mother. And his disciples came and took the body and buried it, and they went and told Jesus."*
*(Matthew 14:1-12)*

WHEN I WAS ONLY 21 years old, I was hired as a deputy sheriff in a smaller sheriff's department here in Oregon. I loved police work, was about to graduate from college, and went through the Oregon Police Academy. I only spent a little over one year at this department, subsequently moving on to a larger one in Portland. But I was there long enough to learn about power. How it corrupts, and how it is misused by those who possess it. The sheriff, who was touted as an up-and-coming young political figure, had his little band of loyalists whom he owed for helping get him elected. On at least two occasions, I came to work and found that one of these people had been promoted to sergeant, and on still another day suddenly here was this new "guy" whom I had never seen before whom the sheriff had hired as a lieutenant! No job openings for these promotions had ever been listed.

Money also changed hands. At year end, remaining budget funds were paid out for "overtime" work, and it was that little circle who received the large bulk of those monies. In the end, this sheriff came crashing down after it became public news that he had taken trustee prisoners from the jail home to do work on his house and that he had made sexual advances toward them. He died of sexually transmitted disease some years later.

The abuse of power. Evil seeks out high places. And therefore, we must not be surprised to find that wickedness seeks out high position in the Christian Church. Church history is filled with such examples, is it not? Man, in his sin, craves to create positions of power, so unbiblical hierarchies and offices are created and then filled with men who have a lust for power and control and, well, that brings us back to abuse, doesn't it? These wolves in sheep's clothing have been responsible for horrid abuse of the people of Christ for centuries, and they do it all in the name of the Jesus whom they persecute.

Yesterday as my wife and I were cruising down the highways on a motorcycle trip, I found myself (as I increasingly am doing) looking at church buildings as we passed them. Many of them have the typical church billboards out front with pithy sayings (many are rather corny and pathetic, but some are good). And what do I think when I see these churches? I find myself wondering, "Is a wolf 'shepherding' the flock there?" "How many victims of secret abuse might there be in that place?" "How many biblical doctrines are distorted in that building every week to serve the pleasure of abusive people?" "Is that place really a local church of Jesus Christ, or has He long since departed?" And, mind you, I am not speaking about the obviously liberal churches that deny the inerrancy and authority of the Scriptures. I know what they are. No, the ones that cause me to wonder and ask these questions are those churches like mine, who profess to believe the Word of God.

Lest anyone think that I am being too critical or exaggerating the case, let me remind our readers that I am regularly contacted by readers who are married to an abuser who is also a pastor. I haven't kept track of the numbers, but given how very difficult it must be for a pastor's wife who is being abused by a husband who is a pastor to admit it to anyone, I believe that the numbers of such pastors is higher than any of us might really want to know. Remember though, evil seeks out high places. "I will be like the Most High" is its craving.

And really then, what better place to exercise that deception and abuse than in the role of pastor? A real shepherd of Christ's flock may not realize this, but the pastoral office, in the hands of wicked men, can be crafted into an incredibly powerful device for exalting the one holding it and for subjecting, using, and abusing those he sets himself over. He speaks God's Word! He tells people how they must live! He hears their confessions and represents them to God! This is how people, if they become gullible and fail to search out the Scriptures, will be brought under the control of a wolf.

And what of such a man's wife? What of "the pastor's wife"? As most any conservative pastor's wife will tell you, being married to the pastor of her church is no picnic, even if he is a genuine, godly man! Incredible pressure can be put upon her, even though she doesn't get a paycheck! In most churches, you'd better believe that she has a job description, though it is an unwritten one. Now, couple all of this with the scenario in which the pastor is an abusive husband, and can you imagine the terrible position his wife is in?

And this brings us back round to John the Baptist. Abuse must be exposed and confronted. I do not mean by this that the abuse victim herself needs to do this, though she will certainly be key in the exposure. We all know by now that there are complicated factors that prevent an abuse victim from just coming "out with it" or "just leaving the jerk!" Children, finances, whether she will be believed or not, physical danger to her and her children at the hands of her abuser, and so on can all limit her ability to confront and expose. But I speak more here to the rest of us. Certainly to all true pastors. John the Baptist saw corruption and the abuse of power in King Herod, and John did not shirk from his duty: "It is not lawful for you to have her." Off to prison he went and ultimately, off came his head.

Confronting abuse is costly, and one reason it is costly is because abuse concerns power and control. Abusers are often in positions of power. Like Satan, they represent evil in high places. Yet we are all called, as God's people, to speak God's truth no matter what the cost. To remain silent about the infection of abuse that exists throughout the church today is to refuse to confess Jesus Christ before men. And that has far more serious and eternal consequences than having your head lopped off.

# 42

# KEEP THE MAIN THING THE MAIN THING

*"But I have this against you, that you have abandoned the love you had at first." (Revelation 2:4)*

ONCE I HEARD ABOUT A CHURCH down in the South (of course – the story involves fried chicken), that started giving cheap fried chicken meals to people in need, or for that matter, anyone who wanted to stop by. As time went along the fame of this chicken spread far and wide. Customer numbers increased, so the church fathers decided to up the price. The thing just kept snowballing and.... well, no one really remembers when it happened. But today, that church building is a fried chicken restaurant. There are just a few vestiges of the Christianity that used to dominate – you see it on the menu here and there – The Goliath (that's a 12-piece bucket), or The Inferno (hot and spicy buffalo wings) – things like that. Profits are big. But the church is no more.

In the history of the Christian church, there are many examples of detour from mission. Most of you have probably heard of liberal Christianity's pursuit of the "Social Gospel," which embraced social reform in place of the preaching of the gospel of Christ. Maybe some things were reformed, but it certainly wasn't done by the power of the gospel –

*"For Christ did not send me to baptize but to preach the gospel, and not with words of eloquent wisdom, lest the cross of Christ be emptied of its power. For the word of*

*the cross is folly to those who are perishing, but to us who are being saved it is the power of God." (1 Cor. 1:17-18)*

As we are involved in this ministry to the victims of abuse, we must always remember to keep the main thing the main thing. The main thing is Christ. The gospel. The main thing is to preach the Word of Christ to people who are lost and perishing in their sin. For those victims we meet who are Christians, we apply the love of Christ in doing everything we can to help them get free and to heal. While we do so in many ways that are similar to secular programs for the abused, we have an incredible thing that they do not have. We have the gospel of Christ and the transforming power of Christ.

It's the same when we deal with victims who don't know Him. Yes, we want to help them, to see them get free from their abuser. But we don't dare stop there. We are commissioned by our Lord to present them with Jesus Christ and the redemption that is in Him. That's the main thing. Because unless a person is set free from the ultimate abuser – the devil – in the end, for all our efforts, they will perish for all eternity.

I think that ministry to victims of abuse is a HUGE mission field. Is it not interesting that the first fruit of the harvest in John chapter four was that Samaritan woman, who may well have been the victim of serial divorce (instead of the harlot she is often thought to have been). And it was just after this that Jesus challenged the disciples –

*"Do you not say, 'There are yet four months, then comes the harvest'? Look, I tell you, lift up your eyes, and see that the fields are white for harvest." (John 4:35)*

So, let's go for it! But take care, lest we become a fried chicken restaurant, devoid of Christ.

# 43

# WE HAVE GONE VERY,
# VERY WRONG

*"But I want you to understand that the head of every man is Christ, the head of a wife is her husband, and the head of Christ is God." (1 Cor. 11:3)*

IF ANYONE THOUGHT that this post was going to be about how those "horrid radical feminists" have attacked and maligned the Bible, well, you are going to be surprised. When I say that we have gone wrong in our teaching of the biblical doctrine of husband as head of his wife – I mean conservative, Bible-believing Christians have gone wrong.

I have been thinking about this matter quite a lot over the last few months, and things just are not settling well with me. To add to my discomfort, I re-read the wonderful article by Steven Tracy last night, "1 Corinthians 11:3: A Corrective to Distortions and Abuses of Male Headship." You can find it online.

Tracy does a great job and in fact calls us to hear at least some of the fundamental charges being made even by radical feminists who flatly hate the Bible. (In some ways I suppose we here in this Unholy Charade community are becoming more and more "radical feminists." By radical however in that context I do not mean the radicalness that rejects Christ and His Word). Primarily however Tracy deals with the Scripture itself and calls us to consider that the Bible teaches an intimate relationship of two equal-in-essence beings in both the Father and Son relationship and in the husband/wife relationship in marriage.

THIS IS THE STUFF THAT WE HAVE FAILED TO SAY FROM OUR PULPITS! And as a result, the biblical truths of the husband as head of the wife as the Father is head of the Son, have been all messed up and misapplied by sinful people like us. It has been made to be a power and control issue when it is not. Power and control in the hands of sinful beings always, always, always carries the likely danger for abuse of that power.

In reading what Tracy had to say, I was also impressed with the fact that it really is true that down through the ages, men have abused their power over women. The thing is undeniable unless a person wants to be willfully blind. When those who hate Christianity shout this charge, we need to stop writing them off and listen. They probably have a point and they have documented it. Those with power inevitably abuse that power and oppress the weak. Guilty.

Think about it. In conservative, Bible-believing churches like ours, men are pastors and elders and deacons and male leadership is endorsed in the home. Do we appreciate the potential for abuse of those positions? I don't think so. We think too highly of ourselves. The result? Well, all you have to do is read the comments and stories in my blog Unholy Charade to find out what the results have been. Abused people, generally women, abused by men – and then further abused by the male leadership of their churches and by the women in those churches who have been taught to go along with the unbiblical traditions and applications of "Scripture."

And you know what? THIS, I believe, is a fundamental reason for all of this cover up and denial we meet with in churches when we try to expose this injustice toward victims. We are assaulting the very power structure of the thing. We are like whistle-blowers. Pastors and church leaders (generally men) panic when an abuse victim comes to them asking for justice. They may not realize that this is the psychological dynamic going on in their heads at the time, but it is there. They are afraid. Afraid of what? Afraid that the system is going to be shown to be broken. Afraid of the consequences of siding with a woman against her husband. Afraid that we all just might have to admit that a bunch of what we have been teaching our churches and our wives and our kids has been a bunch... of bunk!

So, the fear reigns and the victim is given one of those long shepherd hook staff thingies around the neck and dragged off the stage.

# 44

# CLING TO THE GOODNESS OF GOD OR WE ARE UNDONE

*"Of David, when he changed his behavior before Abimelech, so that he drove him out, and he went away. I will bless the LORD at all times; his praise shall continually be in my mouth. My soul makes its boast in the LORD; let the humble hear and be glad. Oh, magnify the LORD with me, and let us exalt his name together! I sought the LORD, and he answered me and delivered me from all my fears. Those who look to him are radiant, and their faces shall never be ashamed. This poor man cried, and the LORD heard him and saved him out of all his troubles. The angel of the LORD encamps around those who fear him, and delivers them. Oh, taste and see that the LORD is good! Blessed is the man who takes refuge in him!" (Psalm 34:1-8)*

THE LORD IS GOOD. He does good for those who fear Him. He is even more than good. He is goodness itself.

The religion of the Pharisees teaches us otherwise and to the degree that we have been infected with its leaven, we are suffering. We must cling to the truth that the Lord is good, or we will be undone. The Pharisaical, abusive counterfeit of Christianity that is so common today – the religion of the Pharisees – teaches us that God is not really good. It teaches us that even those who fear and reverence Him had better fear Him because He is watching and waiting for them to mess up. It teaches us that God is really quite mean and in a bad mood most all the time.

Abusive people, whether they be an abuser spouse or a spiritual abuser in a church, distort our image of the Lord. They tell us that no one, including the Lord, is pleased with us. That the way we dress, or how we talk, or what we like is all downright evil and repugnant. And very often such people put themselves across as speaking for God. And we believe them after a while. They tell us from pulpits. They tell us when they drop by our house. And if you live with one, they tell you all the time. ALL the time.

The thing is one big lie! God is good. He is abounding in lovingkindness toward His people (and He is actually pretty good to His enemies too!). God delights in pouring out good gifts upon His children. He gets a kick out of it. And yet we are told that He really does these things begrudgingly and with much hesitation. He is made out to be the great Celestial Miser.

BUT HE GAVE US HIS SON! How much more will He give us every single gift heaven has to offer (see Ephesians 1).

The Lord puts us all through some pretty trying times. Sometimes, and it can be for quite a long time, He just seems absent. Heaven is silent. We find ourselves in great difficulties and we start to doubt His goodness – if not His very existence. We wonder (with plenty of help from Pharisees around us) if the miserable mess we are in at the moment is ever going to change.

And then it does. Oh, maybe not entirely. Perhaps in just some little way. But though He puts us through trials for the strengthening of our faith in Him and to teach us things that we could never learn apart from those trials, God always, always, always delights in His own. Christian, God is not mad at you. And I will put it in another way that is going to sound a bit shocking to many of you because you have been told the opposite for so long. Here it is:

*A Christian does not deserve hell.*

The religion of the Pharisees says otherwise. Haven't you heard it pretty frequently from people who say they are Christians? "Well, you know, we are all sinners deserving of hell." NO WE ARE NOT! We used to be, but not anymore. In fact, we are no more deserving of Hell than the Son of God Himself – how does that strike you? I can prove it –

*"There is therefore now no condemnation for those who are in Christ Jesus." (Romans 8:1)*

I don't know why God in His perfect wisdom and providence permitted (we Calvinists will even say "decreed") that you would get yourself tied up with a wicked, abusive spouse. I know that God is always without sin – there is no evil in Him. And I know that such evil people will one day give an account, and it won't go well with them. And I also know that God hears the cries of His oppressed people, and that He loves to give them EXODUS.

So don't fall prey to the religion of the Pharisees. It is all around us. It may even sometimes be that entire churches have been totally infected by its leaven. But God is good no matter what Pharisees say. And like any good father, our Father delights in us and takes great joy in doing good for us. Cling to that truth and don't let go of it.

# 45

# HOW THE PHARISEES CREEP IN AMONG US

I AM WORKING RIGHT NOW on the second sermon in my series The Religion of the Pharisees.[7] It hit me hard when I read Galatians 2:4-6 as I had never understood it before. The following paragraphs are from my yet unfinished sermon. Oh man, it's almost Sunday! Anyway, this is really, really good stuff that the Apostle Paul is telling us here:

Our churches are in bondage in many, many cases because the traditions of the Pharisees have been foisted upon us. Their traditions are always abusive, power-hungry lording-it-over in nature, and always put people in bondage. They kill the spirit of a person.

> *"Yet because of false brothers secretly brought in—who slipped in to spy out our freedom that we have in Christ Jesus, so that they might bring us into slavery—to them we did not yield in submission even for a moment, so that the truth of the gospel might be preserved for you. And from those who seemed to be influential (what they were makes no difference to me; God shows no partiality) – those, I say, who seemed influential added nothing to me."* (Galatians 2:4-6)

See it. Pharisees come in amongst God's people secretly and their whole goal is to spy out our freedom that we have in Christ. They want to "catch" us eating what we want, going where we want, reading what we want, living as the Spirit of Christ in us

frees us to live! THE PHARISEE CANNOT STAND OR
TOLERATE FREEDOM!! And what is their goal in this spying?
What do they do with the "data" they gather? They use it to
condemn us, to accuse us, and to bring us into slavery to
themselves in the damning, condemning system that they have
created themselves from their Spiritless handling of the Word of
God.

Also notice carefully that Paul says he did not regard "those
who seemed to be influential" with any partiality. Hear that? One
of the ways that we fall prey to the bondage of the religion of the
Pharisees is that we idolize people who have managed, by hook or
crook, to get themselves exalted in the Christian church. The big
names. The big guns. This is a trap. And I am afraid that we
have gotten ourselves all snared up in it. Remember, it is the
religion of the Pharisees that is very, very often (if not always) at
the root of the abuse that abuse victims are being subjected to by
their churches.

# 46

# Our Inheritance in Christ is for Men and Women

I AM ONLY GOING to cite three Scriptures here in this very short post. They have real significance to the subject of abuse because they concern God's view of women in His kingdom. Specifically, they teach us that women have full rights to all the blessings that are in Christ and are not second-rate beings in His realm. The first Scripture, it appears to me, is really the background to the second and I would imagine that the Apostle Paul had it in mind as he wrote to the Galatians:

> *"Now Zelophehad the son of Hepher, son of Gilead, son of Machir, son of Manasseh, had no sons, but only daughters, and these are the names of his daughters: Mahlah, Noah, Hoglah, Milcah, and Tirzah.*
>
> *They approached Eleazar the priest and Joshua the son of Nun and the leaders and said, "The LORD commanded Moses to give us an inheritance along with our brothers." So according to the mouth of the LORD he gave them an inheritance among the brothers of their father. Thus there fell to Manasseh ten portions, besides the land of Gilead and Bashan, which is on the other side of the Jordan, because the daughters of Manasseh received an inheritance along with his sons. The land of Gilead was allotted to the rest of the people of Manasseh."*
> *(Joshua 17:3-6)*

There are reasons the Lord gives Scriptures like this. Normally, the New Testament explains why. So it is, in my opinion, in this case:

> *"There is neither Jew nor Greek, there is neither slave nor free, there is no male and female, for you are all one in Christ Jesus. And if you are Christ's, then you are Abraham's offspring, heirs according to promise."*
> *(Galatians 3:28-29)*

While I believe that Galatians 3:28 has often been mis-handled, nevertheless it has great application and implications for us today. Just as sons are heirs, so it is with daughters. Peter says the same thing:

> *"Likewise, husbands, live with your wives in an under-standing way, showing honor to the woman as the weaker vessel, since they are heirs with you of the grace of life, so that your prayers may not be hindered."*
> *(1 Peter 3:7)*

Heirs with men, you see. This fact alone sets Christianity poles apart from so many, if not all, religions men have created. Oh, that Christians would just get it!

# 47

## ABUSE AND SECRECY - WHAT HAVE WE GOT TO HIDE?

*"Take no part in the unfruitful works of darkness, but instead expose them." (Ephesians 5:11)*

ONE OF THE REASONS abusers can hide so well in the church is because of our campaign of silence. Let me see if I can explain what I mean.

Scripture tells us that we are to speak well of others, that we are to guard our tongues so as to not slander or gossip. Our speech is to be edifying. There are things we should not speak about. Vulgarity and crude jokes are not to be part of our vocabulary. We all know this.

At the same time, we ARE to speak loudly and clearly when evil needs to be exposed. There is a time not to speak, but there is a time when it is a sin to keep silent. Christ is in the business of exposing evil when it is in His church and He commands all of us to do the same. Announce it to the congregation. Name names. Rebuke publicly when a person refuses to repent, and so on.

But we don't do this. We most commonly keep sin a secret. The details have to be pried out of our mouths. I remember, for example, some years ago when a pastor was discovered to be abusing his wife and living an immoral lifestyle. At an annual meeting of pastors that this man had been a part of, there were hushed comments about "Hey, where is so and so?" "Well, haven't you heard?" Ultimately a written announcement was made that he was no longer a pastor and had left his family. But even in that announcement, cautious words were used: "We are not free to give all of the details. You understand of course. We don't want to say anything improper."

Well, let me ask, "Why?" Sure, there are times when situations require discretion as to what is said and not every single person in the world needs to know every detail. I would hope that such limitations to what is revealed are intended for the good of the victim however, and not for the protection of the guilty man's reputation. Alas, I am afraid that reputation protection – both of the guilty party AND of ourselves – is more often the motivation for this silence.

Ask yourself again: how does Christ handle sin in His church? Does He hush it up? Does he deal with it "quietly and discreetly"? Or does He announce it from the mountaintops? For anyone who knows God's Word this is a no-brainer.

Why do we feel that we have to protect the "sensibilities" of our congregation, sparing them the nasty details of what an abuser has done? Once more, ask yourself – how does the Word of God approach these things? Does it say, "John Smith has failed to love his wife and often speaks to her in anger"? Or does this sound more like God's description: "John Smith has consistently terrorized his wife and children. For years he has raped and sodomized his wife. He has threatened to slit her throat if she ever tells anyone. And all the while, John Smith has been among us as a practiced hypocrite, pretending to be a fine Christian man."

So I ask, why do we cover up. Here are a few suggestions:

1. Reality threatens the fantasyland of "goodness" in which we live.

2. The truth divides. It demands that we decide and take a side. And that means that the comfortable hot-tub environment of our churches will be rocked. People could leave. Money will be lost.

3. We are arrogant. We refuse to admit that such things could happen among us. So we minimize their

severity and then boast about how forgiving we are (all at the expense of the victim of course).

4.  We are foolishly and dangerously naive about evil.

5.  We exalt men's reputations above the name of Christ.

I do not believe that all our talk about avoiding gossip, of not wanting to slander anyone, or of some desire to "protect" people explains the silence about evil in the church. I suggest that this silence stems more often than not from selfish, sinful desire to minimize it, avoid dealing with it, and making it just disappear out of sight.

> *"But I have a few things against you: you have some there who hold the teaching of Balaam, who taught Balak to put a stumbling block before the sons of Israel, so that they might eat food sacrificed to idols and practice sexual immorality. (15) So also you have some who hold the teaching of the Nicolaitans. (16) Therefore repent. If not, I will come to you soon and war against them with the sword of my mouth." (Revelation 2:14-16)*

# 48

# ABUSE AND THE PASTOR'S OFFICE DESK

*"Not that we lord it over your faith, but we work with you for your joy, for you stand firm in your faith." (2 Cor. 1:24)*

I WAS RECENTLY IMPRESSED with the professional demeanor of many pastors and it set my mind working on, you guessed it, abuse. We have all written and read much about how abuse victims are so often cruelly handled by their churches and their church leaders. Much of this malpractice occurs in the pastor's office. I mean, in the literal room where his desk and books are and degree certificates hang on the wall. You go into his office, and if you are a victim of abuse then you go with real trepidation and heart racing, looking for help and answers. There he is, standing and soon to be seated behind his large and impressive desk.

Things matter. Even desks. You know that they do. How do you feel when you walk into an office like that and see the books on shelves behind him? Books you know nothing much about but which apparently hold divine secrets known to studied men? [Let me tell you a secret. Most pastors haven't even begun to read those books on display behind their desk!] I can tell you how you feel. Intimidated. And so would I.

And then, as the session proceeds and you have poured out just a bit of your story of abuse, the pastor behind the big desk, whose name is on those certificates on the wall, begins to expound and counsel. He is confident. He takes off his glasses and polishes them. There is a large, leather-bound Bible laying on his desk right in front of him. He has such an air of confidence as he sorts through its pages. And then he pronounces. You must stay with your abuser. God does not permit divorce. Surely you have over-reacted. He knows your abuser to be a genuine Christian. God takes us all through hard times, but we must be patient. Besides, no doubt you have not been the spouse you should have been either. And think of the children.

Why does this hit you so hard? Why can't victims just "blow it all off" as the nonsense that it is? Well, in part – perhaps largely in part – because of the desk. And by "the desk" I mean all of the trappings in the office, the office itself, the air of the pastor – hold us in a certain awe. Surely this man is no ordinary man. What things must he know and what situations must he deal with in this place? It must be here, on this "holy ground" that he communes with the Lord – those times when his office door says "pastor in conference"? [Reality check: One time I was sitting in just such a pastor's office and he behind his desk. It was a church of some 500 people. This guy was on the career fast track. We talked. Then, his wife came into the office. "Aren't you ready yet! We have been waiting for you for 20 minutes!" He replied, "Yeah, yeah, I'll be there." Welcome to that man's real world. I think that his wife wasn't the real problem].

I am not ridiculing the pastoral calling or ministry. But I am calling upon all of us to consider that things are done in the church that inordinately exalt mere men. Men who could be wrong. Men who are fallible. And when such men are wrong and when they fail, many, many people are harmed. The more we exalt them unduly, the greater the harm.

So here is one very practical suggestion, pastors. Get rid of your desk. Do away with those books lining the wall behind your chair. Most pastors do their best study in a study, not in their office. Ask yourself what it is all about, really? The big desk, the books behind, the framed certificates on the wall. What message are you trying to send to the people who walk through your door? For myself, I did away with that whole scene years ago. My "office" looks more like a comfy living room. Yes, I admit there is still one ordination certificate on the wall. I don't know why. I never look at it anymore and neither does anyone else. I guess I need to stow it too.

Let's all humble ourselves and admit the facts. When it comes to this subject of abuse (and many other topics as well), we do not know hardly anything about it! We didn't learn about it in seminary. So when we set up our "pastor's office" in the traditional manner of desk-books-certificates, and then authoritatively expound on what God says to abuse victims, we have just increased the damage we do exponentially. We evangelicals don't wear clerical collars, but we have our ways of putting them on nevertheless.

> *"So I exhort the elders among you, as a fellow elder and a witness of the sufferings of Christ, as well as a partaker in the glory that is going to be revealed: shepherd the flock of God that is among you, exercising oversight, not under compulsion, but willingly, as God would have you; not for shameful gain, but eagerly; not domineering over those in your charge, but being examples to the flock."* (1 Peter 5:1-3)

# 49

# The Blind Eye of "Nice" People

*"Pay careful attention to yourselves and to all the flock, in which the Holy Spirit has made you overseers, to care for the church of God, which he obtained with his own blood. I know that after my departure fierce wolves will come in among you, not sparing the flock; and from among your own selves will arise men speaking twisted things, to draw away the disciples after them." (Acts 20:28-30)*

YEARS AGO when I was a brand new sheriff's deputy, I was assigned to guard a prisoner in a hospital. In a fit, he had smashed his hand into a concrete wall at the jail and had to have surgery. He later, in another tantrum, pulled the surgical wiring out and the surgeon told him he was just going to have to live with a crippled hand!

While I was guarding him, we handcuffed him to the hospital bed. A nurse came in, old enough to know better, glared at the handcuff, and asked me in a growly tone – "Is that really necessary?" I told her it was. She didn't believe me.

People deny evil. Well, until it comes calling at their own door. I wonder what that nurse's attitude would have been if it was her own daughter whose face this wicked man had smashed (he was incarcerated on felony assault charges). She may have been a nice lady had I known her in other circumstances, but at that moment when she was living out the denial of evil, she was anything but nice. She was, in fact, an ally of evil.

Wickedness exists. There is a devil. Human beings are capable of and indeed commit vicious acts of violence against the image of God every single day. Their throat really is an open grave. There is no fear of God before their eyes. As Paul warned us, even in the church (perhaps especially in the church) wolves are on the prowl. Satan as a roaring lion is lurking just outside the door waiting to pounce. Why in the world do we think these things aren't true? Do we accuse God of exaggeration?

Truly nice people do NOT deny evil. Good people hunger and thirst for righteousness and look forward to justice being done. Nice people do not selfishly isolate themselves in a fantasy land like the Emerald City of Oz (where even the wicked witch sauntered in sometimes). But so often the Christian church acts like a mob of munchkins dancing around the good witch Glenda, singing Ding, Dong the Witch is Dead. No, the witch is not dead! Not yet.

Essentially every single Christian victim of abuse who I have talked to tells me the same thing. Christians – all of these nice people in their churches – intentionally turned a blind eye to the evil that was being done to them when they asked for help. And then, an odd thing happened (which, as it turns out, is really quite logical). The nice people turned nasty. But not against the abuser. No, they turned their guns on the victim for daring to rock their dreamland.

Good people do not deny the reality of evil. Good people are not naive about the tactics of the enemy. Good people rise up in anger against evil when they see it. Good people mirror the image of God, who Himself does all these very things.

All of this is why, quite frankly, I don't like "nice" people. They won't ever have your back. You can't trust them.

*"Let them alone; they are blind guides. And if the blind lead the blind, both will fall into a pit." (Matthew 15:14)*

# 50

# IF A CHURCH BELIEVES THIS,
# RUN FROM IT!

THE FOLLOWING PARAGRAPH is taken from the doctrinal statement of a fundamentalist church. This same church also requires members to acknowledge that the King James Version of the Bible is the divinely preserved Bible to be used by Christians. It also requires members to believe that God created the universe in 6 literal 24-hour days. I believe God did create the universe in that time frame, but do we actually make it a basis of who we consider to be a real Christian to be?

You can bet there will also be, in such a church, all kinds of unwritten "tradition" rules that are exalted to the level of, or even above, Scripture. This kind of an environment creates an abuser-friendly culture in a church, and woe to the abuse victim who tries to get help in such a place.

Here is that church's statement on divorce:

> MARRIAGE, DIVORCE, AND REMARRIAGE: We believe that marriage was instituted by God to be a permanent union between a man and a woman and therefore we are opposed to same sex marriages. We further believe that God hates divorce and intends marriage to last until one of the spouses dies. Divorce and remarriage is regarded as adultery except on the grounds of fornication. Although divorced and remarried persons or divorced persons may hold positions of service in the Church and be greatly used of God for Christian service, they may not be considered for the offices of pastor or deacon (Genesis 2:24; Malachi 2:14-17; Matthew 19:3-12; Romans 7:1-3; I Timothy 3:2, 12; Titus 1:6).

This is a very large church in a large metro area. It isn't just some little oddity, and churches like this can be found rather easily around the country.

# 51

# INSIGHTS FROM ABRAHAM AND SARAH

*"Likewise, wives, be subject to your own husbands, so that even if some do not obey the word, they may be won without a word by the conduct of their wives, when they see your respectful and pure conduct. Do not let your adorning be external–the braiding of hair and the putting on of gold jewelry, or the clothing you wear – but let your adorning be the hidden person of the heart with the imperishable beauty of a gentle and quiet spirit, which in God's sight is very precious. For this is how the holy women who hoped in God used to adorn themselves, by submitting to their own husbands, as Sarah obeyed Abraham, calling him lord. And you are her children, if you do good and do not fear anything that is frightening."*
*(1 Peter 3:1-6)*

I HAVE ESPECIALLY HAD TROUBLE trying to sort out this business of Sarah obeying Abraham, even calling him lord. Most of our readers have no doubt struggled with how to apply this part of God's word in an abuse situation. And many have had it quoted to them, perhaps even by their "Christian" abuser, or at least by fellow Christians. One conclusion I have made is that the phrase "even if some do not obey the word" means simply that a woman finds herself married to an unbeliever. I don't think it means that no matter how sinful and wicked and thus disobedient to God, she must submit to him.

But one of our readers made a comment this week about Abraham that really spurred on my thinking and I think that perhaps it has helped me come to an even better understanding of what Peter means here.

Sarah was married to Abraham. She submitted to him as her husband. But Abraham was Abraham. Not perfect by any means as we know, and yet listen to what the Lord Jesus had to say about him:

> *"I know that you are offspring of Abraham; yet you seek to kill me because my word finds no place in you. I speak of what I have seen with my Father, and you do what you have heard from your father." They answered him, 'Abraham is our father.' Jesus said to them, 'If you were Abraham's children, you would be doing the works Abraham did, but now you seek to kill me, a man who has told you the truth that I heard from God. This is not what Abraham did. You are doing the works your father did.' They said to him, 'We were not born of sexual immorality. We have one Father – even God.'*
>
> *Jesus said to them, 'If God were your Father, you would love me, for I came from God and I am here. I came not of my own accord, but he sent me. Why do you not understand what I say? It is because you cannot bear to hear my word. You are of your father the devil, and your will is to do your father's desires. He was a murderer from the beginning, and has nothing to do with the truth, because there is no truth in him. When he lies, he speaks out of his own character, for he is a liar and the father of lies.'" (John 8:37-44)*

And again:

> *"Your father Abraham rejoiced that he would see my day. He saw it and was glad." (John 8:56)*

Yes, Sarah submitted to Abraham. Yes, Abraham was quite capable of sin, as Scripture tells us. But Abraham loved the Lord. Abraham knew Christ. Abraham did not try to murder the people of God. This is the kind of man then that Peter is talking about. Where in Scripture does the Lord tell a woman to submit to a man who is a child of the devil? Jesus didn't. He called these Pharisees out and told them just what they were.

So, if a woman is married to a man who has the spirit of Abraham, well perhaps then it is quite wise to show patience when he messes up. But I cannot believe that this Scripture or any other was ever meant to be used to force the spouse of a cruel, wicked person to remain in bondage to that person and be forced to obey their whims. Abigail didn't.

# 52

# REPENTANCE AND ABUSE - REAL REPENTANCE BEARS FRUIT

*"Peter, an apostle of Jesus Christ, To those who are elect exiles of the dispersion in Pontus, Galatia, Cappadocia, Asia, and Bithynia, according to the foreknowledge of God the Father, in the sanctification of the Spirit, for obedience to Jesus Christ and for sprinkling with his blood: May grace and peace be multiplied to you." (1Peter 1:1-2)*

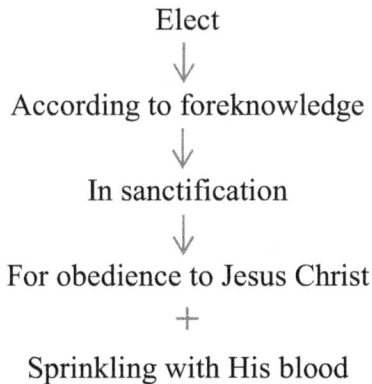

Elect

↓

According to foreknowledge

↓

In sanctification

↓

For obedience to Jesus Christ

+

Sprinkling with His blood

IN THESE FEW WORDS, the Apostle Peter debunks any notion that a person can be a Christian yet not pursue holiness or obey Jesus Christ. The whole chain is linked and flows together. God the Father in eternity past loved His own people (that is what it means to "foreknow." It doesn't mean looking into the future and seeing who would believe), and out of that love elected and chose them. For what? That they would be sanctified by the Holy Spirit. That means set apart as God's own holy people. Made into a holy priesthood.

In accordance with that election and sanctification, they are a people whose purpose is to obey Jesus Christ, being a people cleansed by His own blood. What then is a Christian?[8] A Christian is a person who has been chosen by God, who has been and is being sanctified by God, who obeys Jesus Christ and who has been cleansed and forgiven by Christ's death upon the cross. That's the whole package.

And this, once again, is why we insist that a person who is dominated and characterized by a mentality of power and control, of entitlement to what is essentially worship, who without conscience can enforce his power and control over others through the use of wicked means, is not and cannot be a Christian. You can be sure that where there is no fruit of repentance, there is no repentance. And where there is no repentance, there is no salvation. The fruit borne by real repentance and faith always evidences itself in increasing holiness of life and in obedience to Jesus Christ as evidence of having been cleansed by His blood.

How does a person know if he or she is elect? Follow the chain. Do you see sanctification working itself out in you? Do you see the Spirit of God leading you into increasing holiness of life? Not perfection, mind you. We don't believe in perfectionism in this life or in some supposed second work of the Spirit that claims to give a state of sinlessness. No. But do you sense and see the results of a great battle having begun within you between the sinful flesh and the leading of the Spirit in you. Paul says (Romans 8) that if we are led by the Spirit and if by the Spirit we are putting to death the deeds of the flesh, then we can be sure that we will live. And do you see a heartfelt desire to obey Jesus Christ and an increasing pattern of doing so in your life. If so, then you can be sure that you are one of God's elect ones. And sure enough, this is the very thing that Peter says in his second epistle:

---

[8] The title of a booklet that is a summation of a sermon I once preached is Who is a Christian? You can get a copy on Amazon.

> *"For this very reason, make every effort to supplement your faith with virtue, and virtue with knowledge, and knowledge with self-control, and self-control with steadfastness, and steadfastness with godliness, and godliness with brotherly affection, and brotherly affection with love. For if these qualities are yours and are increasing, they keep you from being ineffective or unfruitful in the knowledge of our Lord Jesus Christ. For whoever lacks these qualities is so nearsighted that he is blind, having forgotten that he was cleansed from his former sins. Therefore, brothers, be all the more diligent to make your calling and election sure, for if you practice these qualities you will never fall. For in this way there will be richly provided for you an entrance into the eternal kingdom of our Lord and Savior Jesus Christ."(2 Pet. 1:5-11)*

We have heard of pastors who tell abuse victims that they must regard their abuser as being a Christian, even though the abuser shows no repentance and his life is characterized by habitual evil. Being baptized or having said a prayer to accept Christ or being a church member does not make anyone a Christian. If it did, then the Bible would have pronounced Esau to be a most eminent saint. Instead, this is what we read about Esau –

> *"See to it that no one fails to obtain the grace of God; that no "root of bitterness" springs up and causes trouble, and by it many become defiled; that no one is sexually immoral or unholy like Esau, who sold his birthright for a single meal. For you know that afterward, when he desired to inherit the blessing, he was rejected, for he found no chance to repent, though he sought it with tears."* (Hebrews 12:15-17)

And is this not the very thing that so many of our readers have seen and had their fill of in the case of their abuser who claims to be a Christian? Sexual immorality, despising of the grace of God, yet seeking, even with zeal and tears, to be pronounced by God and everyone else to be a true Christian? Such actions alone only qualify a man to be an Esau and nothing more. So, let's not be deceived by a counterfeit repentance that bears only rotten fruit.

We conclude with these great words from J.C. Ryle on Repentance: [Old Paths, Banner of Truth, 1999, Chapter 16] –

> True repentance, such as I have just described, is never alone in the heart of any man. It always has a companion – a blessed companion. It is always accompanied by lively FAITH in our Lord and Savior Jesus Christ. Wherever faith is, there is repentance; wherever repentance is, there is always faith. I do not decide which comes first – whether repentance comes before faith, or faith before repentance. But I am bold to say that the two graces are never found separate, one from the other. Just as you cannot have the sun without light, or ice without cold, or fire without heat, or water without moisture – so long you will never find true faith without true repentance, and you will never find true repentance without lively faith. The two things will always go side by side.

> And now, before I go any further, let us search and try our own hearts, and see what we know about true repentance. I do not affirm that the experience of all penitent people tallies exactly, precisely, and minutely. I do not say that any man ever knows sin, or mourns for sin, or confesses sin, or forsakes sin, or hates sin, perfectly, thoroughly, completely, and as he ought. But this I do say, that all true Christians will recognize something which they know and have felt, in the things which I have just been saying. Repentance, such as I have described, will be, in the main, the experience of every true believer. Search, then, and see what you know of it in your own soul.

> Beware that you make no mistake about the nature of true repentance. The devil knows too well the value of that precious grace not to dress up spurious imitations of it. Wherever there is good coin there will always be bad money. Wherever there is a valuable grace, the devil will put in circulation counterfeits and shams of that grace, and

try to palm them off on men's souls. Make sure that you are not deceived.

# HOW TO IDENTIFY
# THE ABUSE OF POWER

*"Masters, do the same to them, and stop your threatening,
knowing that he who is both their Master and yours is in
heaven, and that there is no partiality with him." (Eph. 6:9)*

POWER (and even control) is not evil in itself. God is omnipotent.
He possesses all power so that whatever power we see in this
world owes its origin to Him. He holds all things together by the
word of His power (Heb 1:3). It is by His power that we are raised
in Christ and made alive and it is this power that enables the King
of kings to destroy all that opposes Him. His Word is accomp-
anied by His power so that it is alive and works within us. So, we
must be thankful for power and not reject it as some kind of "dirty
word" due to its abuse by evil men.

Abusers abuse because they abuse power, and they do so for
control. God cannot abuse His power. He need not fight to gain
control over anything because in His omnipotence He always has
complete control over the smallest molecule in creation. No rebel
in all of history has ever succeeded in escaping the control of
God. This is why God laughs over all such attempts:

*"Why do the nations rage and the peoples plot in vain?
The kings of the earth set themselves, and the rulers take
counsel together, against the LORD and against his
Anointed, saying, 'Let us burst their bonds apart and cast
away their cords from us.' He who sits in the heavens
laughs; the Lord holds them in derision."(Psalm 2:1-4)*

When power is abused, the abuser fails to acknowledge that any power he possesses is delegated by and originates in the Lord. Authority and power never originate in creatures, so that no man can say "I am entitled to power and control" simply by virtue of who they are. No, all power and all authority is from and of the Lord and it is only given so that it might be used for the glory of God and the good of human beings. Abusers deny all of this and see themselves as gods.

As I read the verse quoted above (Ephesians 6:9) I was impressed with that word "threatening." God requires masters of slaves (slavery having been widespread in New Testament times) to exercise the authority and power they have been given over slaves in a righteous manner. While "threatening" is, once again, not evil in itself (because God certainly threatens the wicked quite often in Scripture), it is not to characterize the master's authority over his slaves. He is not to "lord it over" those under his power and he is to remember that one day the ground will be very level when Christ comes to hold all accountable.

But what impressed me in particular about this idea of power and "threatening" is that this verse appears in the context of other relationships: fathers and children, husbands and wives. And surely the instruction given to masters of slaves must also apply to fathers and to husbands – to those with power in other words. They are not to abuse this power. They must not be characterized by threatening. And therefore, I would suggest that herein we find a tool for identifying the abuse of power. Is it characterized by threatening?

I think that we must understand that this "threatening" that is to be rejected by all who possess power is of a particular nature. Parents, for example. threaten their children, right? "Jimmy, I have asked you to clean up your room twice now. If you don't obey, then there are going to be consequences." [Our two-year old grandson asked his dad, "and what will those consequences be?" Ha!] Certainly there is nothing wrong with that kind of threatening. Or the master of a slave (employee today), in times past, could let a lazy slave know that continued laziness was not going to be tolerated and would have consequences. So, what then is this "threatening" that Paul prohibits those in power from using? Let's look at the context:

> *"Slaves, obey your earthly masters with fear and trembling, with a sincere heart, as you would Christ, not by the way of eye-service, as people-pleasers, but as servants of Christ, doing the will of God from the heart, rendering service with a good will as to the Lord and not to man, knowing that whatever good anyone does, this he will receive back from the Lord, whether he is a slave or free. Masters, do the same to them, and stop your threatening, knowing that he who is both their Master and yours is in heaven, and that there is no partiality with him."*
> *(Ephesians 6:5-9)*

The thing seems contradictory at first glance, right? Here, Paul tells slaves "obey your earthly masters with fear and trembling." Doesn't that encourage the very "threatening" that Paul prohibits? Well, notice that Paul also tells the slaves to obey with fear and trembling, as you would obey Christ…as servants of Christ doing the will of God from the heart…rendering service…as to the Lord and not to man. In other words, the "fear and trembling" is not directed toward the master, but toward the Lord. It is the Lord whom we are to fear and tremble before, and thus, sincerely obey. Therefore, when Paul tells masters to stop their threatening, I suggest that he means stop exercising power over your slaves in such a way that you instill in them fear of yourself and of what you will do to them if they do not do what you tell them.

Think about this. This means that when power is abused, the abuser enforces his will upon his victim by threatening them with what the abuser himself is going to do to them if they do not comply. And it is his will that is enforced, not the Lord's. "Get out there and fix my dinner right or I will…." and so on. There is no fear of the Lord involved in the thing. And even when parents threaten their children with consequences for disobedience, they must remind the children that ultimately it is the Lord whom they are disobeying, and it is the Lord who will one day judge us all. Power is abused when the Lord is left out of the equation and when those with power threaten their victims with what the abuser himself will do if the victim does not concede to the abuser's own selfish and wicked demands. Thus, the victim does not comply out of fear of the Lord, but out of the fear of man.

The abuse of power then can be identified by its inevitable use of this selfish, godless threatening. All of us would do well to examine our own hearts and words and actions for this evil threatening. Put this test question to yourself: does my leadership instill the fear of the Lord in those under my charge, or are they primarily fearful of me? Because, you see, when human beings speak of "I am going to put the fear of God in that woman/kid/employee," almost always the fear of God has nothing to do with it at all. What is really meant is "I am going to teach them to fear me."

I suspect we will find that we turn to making people afraid of us far more often than we might like to admit. And abusers do this habitually. If you want a real humbling challenge, go ask your wife, your children, your employees, this question: "Are you afraid of me?" I think in many cases the answer might shock us.

# 54

# YOU MUST LISTEN TO ME!

*"I have written something to the church, but Diotrephes, who likes to put himself first, does not acknowledge our authority." (3 John 1:9)*

ABUSERS, AS MOST ALL OF YOU KNOW through years of grievous experience, possess a mentality of incredible entitlement. One of the typical displays of this is their insistence that everyone listen to them. Hear what they say. Do what they command, and so on. No doubt Diotrephes was one of these wicked ones. Everyone was to listen to him, not to the apostles. I sure would have liked to have been present when John arrived and took care of this guy for all to see!

I remember dealing with such a person who evidenced this very kind of presumption. "If you had only listened to me." "Look what has happened because you didn't listen to me." "I told my wife that she must obey me." It didn't matter that a whole group of people disagreed with this fellow and considered what he said to be wrong. Nope. They all should have listened to him.

Whether a person like this is operating in a family or in a church, his expectation is the same – everyone must listen to him for true wisdom and anyone who does not is an idiot or rebel. It doesn't really matter what the topic is, HE is to be listened to and obeyed. His lust for power and control is rabid, and like a rabid dog he will attack viciously anyone who fails to hear him.

You can see how this demand that he be listened to and obeyed plays right along with the abuser's insistence that he is never wrong.

It still amazes me to think back to the times when I have seen this evil play itself out right in front of me. Here sits a man, clearly and plainly in the wrong, in sin, being confronted by a group of people who have finally caught on to his devious tactics. Yet he will not admit wrong. He will look up at everyone, often playing the poor wronged victim, and tell them all, "you should have listened to me."

Well, we did listen to him. For many years we listened to him. But no more. Now we know who and what he is.

# 55

# IS IT YOU, YOU TROUBLER
## OF ISRAEL?

*"But Jehoshaphat said, 'Is there not here another prophet of the LORD of whom we may inquire?' And the king of Israel said to Jehoshaphat, 'There is yet one man by whom we may inquire of the LORD, Micaiah the son of Imlah; but I hate him, for he never prophesies good concerning me, but always evil.' And Jehoshaphat said, 'Let not the king say so.'" (2 Chronicles 18:6-7)*

*"When Ahab saw Elijah, Ahab said to him, 'Is it you, you troubler of Israel?' And he answered, 'I have not troubled Israel, but you have, and your father's house, because you have abandoned the commandments of the LORD and followed the Baals.'" (1 Kings 18:17-18)*

WICKED KING AHAB hated the godly prophet Micaiah. And Ahab hated Elijah as well. Why? Because both prophets spoke the truth. God's truth. Notice that Ahab knew full well that these prophets were indeed prophets of God and what they said was in fact God's Word. Didn't matter. Ahab was evil. Ahab didn't want light. So he imprisoned Micaiah and he called Elijah a troublemaker.

We see the very same dynamic here at Unholy Charade, and you all have seen it in your dealings with the abuser, and with the abuser's allies – including so often, pastors and churches. The abuse victim is depicted as the troubler of Israel. She says things that are not "good prophecies concerning her abuser." The thing is troubling. It is unpleasant. These words don't tickle ears. "No more! Tell us no more!"

I have seen this in our church over the years. Wickedness is detected among us. We shine the light of truth on it. Allies of the evil one don't like it and they start accusing – "you are causing unnecessary trouble! You need to be more patient. You are too harsh. We have to love these people to Jesus." You've heard it. But we answer as Elijah answered: "We have not troubled this church, but you have…because you have abandoned the commandments of the Lord."

Abuse victims are not the troublers of Israel. They are not troublers of their families, or of their churches, or of their marriages. The abuser is the troublemaker. His allies, including people in his local church who protect and enable him – they are the troublemakers. So let the Ahabs of our day scream and yell their accusations all they want, the fact is that the reason they are so enraged against the victim is that they are walking in sin, disobeying Christ whose command is that we protect the weak, the widow, the oppressed, and that we shake the dust of abuserville off our feet. And when people abandon the commandments of the Lord, they should expect that God's people will not be prophesying good about them.

# 56

# IS IT OK TO FLEE FROM PERSECUTION?

*"Behold, I am sending you out as sheep in the midst of wolves, so be wise as serpents and innocent as doves. Beware of men, for they will deliver you over to courts and flog you in their synagogues, and you will be dragged before governors and kings for my sake, to bear witness before them and the Gentiles. When they deliver you over, do not be anxious how you are to speak or what you are to say, for what you are to say will be given to you in that hour. For it is not you who speak, but the Spirit of your Father speaking through you.* **Brother will deliver brother over to death, and the father his child, and children will rise against parents and have them put to death***, and you will be hated by all for my name's sake. But the one who endures to the end will be saved.* **When they persecute you in one town, flee to the next***, for truly, I say to you, you will not have gone through all the towns of Israel before the Son of Man comes." (Matt. 10:16-23)*

MANY TIMES we are presented with a false, unbiblical doctrine of suffering that tells us that the Lord always requires us to submit to it and not escape it. Taking scriptures that speak of how the Lord uses suffering in our lives for our growth and for His glory, these distortions of those scriptures make them absolute laws which always apply in every case. And, of course, we see this in the pressure that is put upon victims of abuse by their fellow believers. The victim is told that suffering at the hands of her abuser is the Lord's calling for her. That she is to stay in it and know that she is bringing praise to Christ by being faithful to her marriage covenant, just as Christ is faithful to His Bride, the church (an obviously false parallel if we would think about it for even a few moments).

But there are numbers of Scriptures that show us it is perfectly within the will of God for us to flee from abuse. You could think, for instance, of the times that Jesus Himself departed from crowds who wanted to kill Him. Or of Paul being lowered over the city wall in Damascus, or of his appeal to Caesar when another mob would have killed him. And then we have this scripture here in Matthew 10 that even goes so far as to tell us that we should flee when persecution comes... even if the persecutor is a brother, a father, or one of our own children! The other Scriptures that instruct children to obey their parents are trumped by this passage in a sense because no parent has the right to abuse and persecute his child. When they persecute you in one town, flee to the next.

Some readers might question this application with the observation that Matthew 10 is addressing persecution for the sake of Christ, not out of some quest for the abuser's power and control. But is there really any difference? Furthermore, I maintain that many, many cases of abuse are indeed motivated by hatred of the victim for her love for Christ. Flee! That is Jesus' instruction.

One final thought for our readers to "chew on." Please do not interpret this as a criticism of victims who are still with their abuser – getting away is just not as easy as just "leaving the jerk." But here is a thought that is meant to help them to freedom. Is it not possible that fleeing from the abuser's persecution is a better testimony for Christ than mistakenly thinking that by remaining in the abuse the victim is somehow bringing more glory to Christ? Drawing boundaries and/or leaving is a statement that "this is not a good picture of Christ's love for His Bride." "Fleeing to the next city" also serves to free up the victim so that she is enabled to do an even better job of living for and proclaiming Christ to others.

# 57

# DON'T LISTEN TO THESE LIES

I AM NOT GOING to say anything new in this post. You have all heard it before. But we need to hear it, before, now, and again and again.

An abuse victim who has been targeted not only by her abuser, but by her family members, by her pastor, by the pastor's wife (I need to write a post about pastor's wives and how they so often enable the abuser), and by other church members in her church, told me some of the things she is being told:

- Give him a chance.

- We must forgive people.

- He wants you back.

- He is hurting.

- Stop running from your problems.

- The Bible says for better or worse.

- Stop feeling sorry for yourself.

Now, this stuff just makes my blood boil. Lies. All lies. Let me make a few observations and I imagine you all will have some also –

- Give him a chance – that is what the victim HAS been doing, often for decades! Yeah, give him a chance to abuse and destroy you all over again.

- We must forgive people – Really? Does God forgive everyone? Does God forgive when there is no repentance? NO! Does forgiveness necessitate reconciliation? NO!

- He wants you back – Oh man, you can't invent this stuff. Yes, he wants her back alright. So, his kingdom reign of power and control can be reinstituted in full measure.

- He is hurting – Oh really. So, this means that the people saying these things to the victim have been in contact with the abuser, listening to his plays for pity. They are his allies now. He is hurting? Well how about the victim's hurts? How is it no one seems to even think about how she has suffered? This is pure EVIL.

- Stop running from your problems – Ok, well, the next time someone points a gun at your head, or puts poison in your drink, don't run. Just stand there. Just drink up. And the fact is, abuse victims who leave their abuser, who start calling him on his evil, ARE ceasing to run from their problems! They are now facing those problems square on.

- The Bible says for better or worse – Now this is rich. I will give $1000 to any of these people who can show me chapter and verse on that one. You see, people take statements made by man and they hear it so often in sermons, and in their laziness, they don't check it out, and pretty soon they elevate it to the Word of God. In addition, "for better or worse" was never meant to mean "you must endure even the cruelest wickedness from your spouse no matter what."

- Stop feeling sorry for yourself – Time to get a clue. The person who is feeling sorry for himself is not the victim. It is the abuser. WE must stop feeling sorry for him because his pity ploys are largely how he enlists us as his allies.

To people who lay this cruel garbage on victims, I say go. Just go. Go away and learn what God means when He says He desires mercy, not sacrifice. Close your lips. In the meanwhile, we are done listening to you.

# 58

# THIS SCRIPTURE APPLIES
## TO THE WICKED

*"I appeal to you, brothers, to watch out for those who cause divisions and create obstacles contrary to the doctrine that you have been taught; avoid them. For such persons do not serve our Lord Christ, but their own appetites, and by smooth talk and flattery they deceive the hearts of the naive." (Romans 16:17-18)*

MANY TIMES, people who seek justice in their local churches are accused of being "divisive." They are told they need to be quiet because they are disrupting the "unity" of the church. Verses like the one quoted above are often cited in support of such silencing.

Wrong. Dead wrong.

Victims do not cause divisions in the body of Christ. The wicked do. And when the church refuses to effect justice in obedience to what Paul is teaching here in Romans 16, the church is guilty of causing division. Seeking justice for evil done does not cause division in Christ's church. It promotes unity! It addresses the real culprit, the real one causing division and creating obstacles.

Verse 18 really sheds light on what kind of person verse 17 is speaking of. Who have we seen over and over again use "smooth talk and flattery" in order to deceive and to obtain self-serving objects? Who? Who are they? The victims of abuse? NO! It is the abuser who pulls these tactics and who has these things as his goal. HE is the one who is causing divisions and obstacles. HE is the one we are all to watch out for and AVOID.

The victim who seeks justice is not the source of division in a church. The source is the wicked man and the disobedient church that allies with him because they like his smooth talk and flattery.

> *"Take no part in the unfruitful works of darkness, but instead expose them." (Ephesians 5:11)*

Fail in this regard, fail to avoid the wicked divider of Christ's people, embrace him and his flattery and accuse the victim who seeks justice of causing division, and you have just taken part in the unfruitful works of darkness. YOU molested that child. YOU abused that abuse victim. How? Because you refused to expose them, and by default such refusal renders YOU a participant in those evil works.

Yep.

# 59

# HOW ABUSERS SELECT A TARGET - LASER DOT ON

CROSS-HAIRS. Laser sights. Bulls-eyes. FIRE! Abusers have targets. They select them. They keep them in their sights. Abuse victims can probably identify with the image of living every day, moment by moment, with a laser dot on their forehead, heart, or back. A constant reminder that a shot could be fired any second. For any reader who hasn't actually been an abuser's target, perhaps this imagery will help you understand the nature of this evil better, and the effects it has upon a victim-target. Think about it. What kind of effects might you experience if there were a red laser targeting dot on you every single day?

I don't know specifically what the psychology is of abuser target selection. I just know that they do it. Scanning, scanning, target acquired! Locked on! Once they press the fire button and the missile is launched, life for the target becomes something akin to a pilot with a heat-seeking missile chasing after him. Evasive action constantly required! Hyper-vigilance.

Perhaps the abuser's target selection is something like this:

1. Mentality of entitlement to have power and control over.

2. Sighting of someone who, the abuser muses, thinks they have power and control over their life, or, sighting someone (i.e., Jesus in the Pharisees' sights) who is perceived as a threat to the abuser's power and control. "You may be the pastor, but I am in charge around here." (Once I had such a person tell me, with his arm around my shoulder, "Jeff, the old pastor used to come out to my farm every Monday and we would talk things

over and decide things." I told him that wasn't going to happen. That was 20 years ago. He still hates me to this day. Small town. Glares).

3. Abuser resolves to conquer – target selected.

In my experience, abusers have shown up in the churches that I have pastored. Many of them have selected me as their target. Why? Because in their warped perception of what a pastor's role is (and believe me, to them it is anything but being a servant), they see someone who preaches, who teaches, who leads. They see a person who…has power and control. They must have it. They must conquer. They must control the pastor and thus the flock. Laser dot on target. In your experience perhaps you were targeted because some sociopath decided "there is a beautiful woman who thinks she is free. I will conquer and control her."

Many of these people  perhaps even most of them  approach us with an unusual charm. I have learned to beware. I am sure that the elders I work with have often wondered "When is Jeff going to learn?" They have been wiser than me in this regard. I hope I have learned, but I still must watch my tendency to be too trusting of charmers. Largely now however, they make me suspicious. When a new person begins to ask for special attention, I wonder "Is this just another abuser/user who wants to 'get next to the pastor' in order to control?" Be very, very careful about giving such a person too much information about yourself. It just makes you an easier target. (Someone told me once that a new pastor should beware of the person who picks him up at the airport).

How can we set up defenses against targeters? One of the most effective means is for us to learn a firm sense of drawing boundaries, and then do it. We need to learn to say "no" to people early on. This one little word can do more to prevent future trouble than almost anything else – "No." We would be wise to test all of our relationships with it. Anyone who literally "cannot take no for an answer" is an unsafe person.

It certainly is not our fault when we are targeted. But by using some wisdom, by growing wise to the tactics of evil, we can go a long way in protecting ourselves from that laser dot.

When we become a difficult target, abusers may very well just decide to move on and find someone who is more of a "sitting duck."

# 60

# MICROSCOPIC BIBLE STUDY CAN LEAD TO MADNESS

*"When the disciples reached the other side, they had forgotten to bring any bread. Jesus said to them, 'Watch and beware of the leaven of the Pharisees and Sadducees.' And they began discussing it among themselves, saying, 'We brought no bread...'"(Matthew 16:5-7)*

*"Then they understood that he did not tell them to beware of the leaven of bread, but of the teaching of the Pharisees and Sadducees." (Matthew 16:12)*

HERE WE HAVE THE DISCIPLES in personal contact with the Lord Jesus, and He speaks to them. "Watch and beware of the leaven of the Pharisees and Sadducees." They analyzed His words. They discussed what he said among themselves. They concluded from their exposition: He is admonishing us for bringing no bread. They were, of course, quite wrong.

In seminary and in our churches, we are taught to minutely examine the Scriptures. The Christian is to be a careful student of the Word of God. Pastors are taught Greek and Hebrew and theology. We memorize the books of the Bible, catechisms, and portions of Scripture.

And quite often, we go wrong.

It is of course the very thing the Pharisees did. They ended up turning a blessing of God – the Sabbath – into a horrid burden so that people couldn't even enjoy what God meant to be body and soul-refreshing rest. Jesus rebuked them for it all – the Sabbath was made for man, not the other way around. We have often said on this blog that, so it is with marriage. Marriage was made for man, not man for marriage. Marriage is not to become some kind of master to which human beings are enslaved. And yet, as we all know, that is the very thing that so many pastors and churches and theologians and books are teaching today. Marriage is the thing. People are subservient to marriage. It is vital that the marriage survive, even if the people don't.

Let me suggest to you a principle that we very much need to add to our hermeneutics tool shop (hermeneutics is what we call the discipline of Bible study and interpretation). Here it is – though I am sure it is in no way original with me:

> *When our conclusions we arrive at through our study of Scripture lead us to ridiculous, unjust interpretations and applications that are not consistent with the character of God, it is time to go back to our study and see where we went wrong.*

It's like a mathematics test. The professor says, "Show your work on your paper so that if you get a wrong answer I can see where you went wrong, and you can go back and correct yourself at that point."

Now really, who can deny in all honesty that the "company line" of no divorce for abuse is a ridiculous, foolish, and dangerous biblical interpretation that is inconsistent with the character of God? It's time for a lot of people who are teaching this stuff to be called out on it and sent back to their homework to correct their work.

Someone is saying "but the no divorce for abuse is NOT ridiculous!" Really? Let me paint a picture [Trigger warning, descriptions of abuse]:

> *Sally has been married to John for 24 years. Sally's life in this marriage has been a living hell. John professes to not only be a Christian, but to be an exemplary student of God's Word and one of the finest pillars in his church. But John terrorizes Sally and the children behind the scenes.*

*Tomorrow, John is going to step up the intensity of his abuse because Sally told him she wants a divorce. John is going to carry out one of the following scenarios (you choose one of them):*

*a) John is going to corner Sally in the bedroom, smash her up against the wall when she doesn't see it coming, put his hands tightly around her neck while he keeps her pinned there, look right into her eyes and in a demonically cold and evil tone, he is going to tell her that if she leaves him he will kill the children and then her. He will find her wherever she is. She and the children are his property and no one is going to take them away from him.*

*b) John knows that Sally is going to divorce him and try to take the children with her. He is not going to allow it. She is a wicked, ungodly woman who will not submit to him and therefore is in rebellion against the Lord. John has tried and tried, but she will not listen to him. Well, if he can't have the kids, then no one can. John takes his 9mm handgun out of the closet and when Sally comes home with the children from the grocery store, he is going to be waiting for them in the living room. He is going to kill them all. John carries these murders out, then gets in the car and speeds down the road thinking about killing himself. Before he can do so however, he is taken into custody by the police.*

What John would soon learn is that the bullet that struck Sally did not kill her. Sally survived, now having to endure this hell on earth without her children.

John Piper, Jim Ellif, Voddie Baucham and others of the "no-divorce-for-any-reason" school would most certainly tell Sally that God does not permit her to divorce this murderer. But the hermeneutical craziness doesn't end with Piper, Ellif and Baucham. Oh no. It goes on. All the pastors and churches and professing Christians who insist that only adultery and a very specific kind of desertion (the literal leaving of an unbelieving spouse married to a believer) are biblical grounds for divorce will tell Sally the very same thing. "Nope. Uh-uh. Can't divorce him. If you do you will be a covenant breaker and sinning before God." Now of course, if John had been an adulterer, no problem, these guys would say. Divorce is ok for that, but not for murder of the children. Others continue teaching this insanity by saying that the desertion rule doesn't apply in this case because that is only specifically for the scenario where an unbeliever refuses to live with a believer. "And after all," these people will tell Sally, "Your husband John professed to be a Christian. Oh sure, he murdered the children and shot you, but hey, King David did a lot of bad stuff too and God stuck with him."

## IT IS TIME TO STOP THE MADNESS!

All of you out there in Christianity Land, listen! This is cruel insanity. This is totally inconsistent with the very character of God as He reveals Himself in Scripture and in the Living Word, His Son. As you all argue over the minute details of Scripture, checking out verb tenses, participles and prepositions, you have come to conclusions that Christ never taught. And instead of saying, "Hmmm....you know, maybe the propeller goes on the front of this plane and not down below on the axle," you absolutely insist that you are going to fly that plane with the wheel where the prop is supposed to be, and you are demanding that all the rest of us get in that plane with you.

Well, we aren't going to. We are finished doing that. You aren't a qualified pilot. And more and more and more you are going to hear loud voices saying so.

# IS NOUTHETIC COUNSELING APPROPRIATE

*"I could not help but notice that the more directive I became (simply telling counselees what God required of them), the more people were helped. Spelling out and getting commitments to biblical patterns of behavior after an acknowledgement of and repentance for sin seemed to bring relief and results."* [9]

*"Apart from those who had organic problems, like brain damage, the people I met in the two institutions in Illinois were there because of their own failure to meet life's problems. To put it simply, they were there because of their unforgiven and unaltered sinful behavior."* [10]

*"The thesis of this book is that qualified Christian counselors properly trained in the Scriptures are competent to counsel – more competent than psychiatrists or anyone else."* [11]

*"The reason why people get into trouble in their relationships to God and others is because of their sinful natures. Men are born sinners."* [12]

JAY ADAMS in his widely circulated book *Competent to Counsel*, lays out his counseling model which he calls **nouthetic counseling**. He draws the name from a New Testament Greek word used in,

---

[9] Jay Adams, *Competent to Counsel*
[10] Ibid.
[11] Ibid.
[12] Ibid.

for example, Colossians 1:28. "We proclaim him confronting every man nouthetically, and teaching every man with all wisdom in order that we may present every man complete in Christ." Adams goes on to say that nouthetic counseling consists of three fundamental elements –

- Nouthetic confrontation necessarily suggests first of all that there is something wrong with the person who is to be confronted nouthetically. The idea of something wrong, some sin, some obstruction, some problem, some difficulty, some need that has to be acknowledged and dealt with, is central. In short, nouthetic confrontation arises out of a condition in the counselee that God wants changed.

- The second element of nouthetic confrontation is that problems are solved nouthetically by verbal means. Nouthetic confrontation, in its biblical usage, aims at straightening out the individual by changing his patterns of behavior to conform to biblical standards.

- The third element in nouthetic confrontation implies changing that in his life which hurts the counselee. "Instead of excuse-making or blame-shifting, nouthetic counseling advocates the assumption of responsibility and blame, the admission of guilt, the confession of sin, and the seeking of forgiveness in Christ."

Let's think about this model through the lens of abuse. Imagine an abuse victim, suffering the effects of ongoing, intense trauma (PTSD), coming to such a counselor. Is her behavior and thinking to be attributed to sin? Yes. But WHOSE sin? Hers? Hardly. Oh yes, as Christians with the sinful flesh still remaining, victims of abuse are certainly prone to unbiblical thinking about what has or is happening to them. They can respond sinfully like all of us can when we are wronged. But is that their chief problem? No. The problem is that these are wounded, traumatized people. Would we counsel a person who has lost their legs in a traumatic car accident that their injury is due to their own sin? Yet somehow, correct me if I am wrong, this is how Adams' nouthetic counseling model communicates to me. Sin! Counter with Truth! Change of thinking! Problem solved, counseling success!

Here is still another troublesome aspect of Adams' model –

*"This is one reason why properly equipped ministers may make excellent counselors. A good seminary education rather than medical school or a degree in clinical psychology, is the most fitting background for a counselor."* [13]

I absolutely agree that if a pastor (or any person) possesses true godly wisdom and knowledge of the Scriptures, that person will be competent to counsel. However, as the sad treatment so commonly dealt to abuse victims in our churches, often at the hands of pastors, demonstrates – good seminary educations do not ensure wisdom. (And, I might add, "good" seminary educations are very hard to come by these days). Pastors emerge from seminary most commonly quite ignorant of the nature and dynamics of evil in general and abuse particularly – which is really to say, they are ignorant of the nature and dynamics of sin. I can say that because I was one of them. Oh, we learned facts about sin – but we never heard about the cunning, evil, scheming nature and strategies of sin that we would face in our churches. That is why many of the graduates have long since crashed and burned in the ministry – or become puppets of abusive, manipulative, narcissistic individuals in their churches.

I would submit that a good seminary education, supplemented by studies in clinical psychology would be an excellent choice for ministry preparation. Those of us who have been pastors for 30 or 40 years have studied clinical psychology in the front lines. We have survived only by the protection of Christ and have had our

[13] Jay Adams, *Competent to Counsel*

thinking enlightened by His Spirit as to the nature of evil. This was a much longer and more difficult course of study. But perhaps it was the better one. Not even a PhD in clinical psychology can give the lessons that years of being in the battle can.

I am not an expert in nouthetic counseling. I am not widely read in the subject. And I do not ever intend to be. But I have read enough of Jay Adams' writings, now that I have studied abuse, to have some serious reservations about this model of counseling – especially in dealing with victims of abuse, or any case of PTSD. Who would this model be more appropriate for? As you read what I have said in this article, many of you may have been thinking – "Yeah, this is the way we should deal with the ABUSER, but certainly NOT with the victim." I agree.

If you want to see an example of my concern, get a copy of Adams' book, *From Forgiven to Forgiving: Learning to Forgive One Another God's Way*, and read chapter 12. There you will find Adams describing how a pastor should deal with a wife whose husband has committed adultery. She initially and too quickly told her husband that she would not divorce him but has now changed her mind. The ensuing "counseling session" conducted by the pastor, with the husband present, is really nothing short of bullying this woman into remaining in the marriage. She, in other words, is really treated as the problem. Her husband, because he has run to the safety zone of, "Gee, honey, I'm sure sorry" – gets off the hook. Adams seems to agree with this rule.

# 62

# WE ALL HAVE THE RIGHT TO CHOOSE OUR FRIENDS

*"Do not be unequally yoked with unbelievers. For what partnership has righteousness with lawlessness? Or what fellowship has light with darkness? What accord has Christ with Belial? Or what portion does a believer share with an unbeliever? What agreement has the temple of God with idols? For we are the temple of the living God; as God said, 'I will make my dwelling among them and walk among them, and I will be their God, and they shall be my people. Therefore go out from their midst, and be separate from them, says the Lord, and touch no unclean thing; then I will welcome you, and I will be a father to you, and you shall be sons and daughters to me, says the Lord Almighty.'" (2 Corinthians 6:14-18)*

I BELIEVE THAT BY FAR AND LARGE, churches and Christians and pastors and teachers are denying the truth of this Scripture. What are we told? We are told that because Jesus loves everyone (by the way, He doesn't!) then we are bound to love everyone, and that love means that we are required to maintain relationship with everyone who asks us. I think this is why you are seeing books come out like *Boundaries* and *Unsafe People*. We are trying to get back the freedom that has been stolen from us.

Christian, YOU have the right to choose your relationships. Did you know that? Have you been taught just the opposite in your church or by other Christians? You do not have to be in a relationship with the "unclean." Of course, we know this does not mean that a Christian who is already married to a non-Christian is commanded to leave that marriage (see 1 Cor 7). But it does mean that in our lives we do not have to be bound together with darkness and those who represent it.

> *"Do not be deceived: 'Bad company ruins good morals.'"* *(1 Corinthians 15:33)*

> *"Whoever walks with the wise becomes wise, but the companion of fools will suffer harm." (Proverbs 13:20)*

> *"Make no friendship with a man given to anger, nor go with a wrathful man, lest you learn his ways and entangle yourself in a snare." (Proverbs 22:24-25)*

Now, whenever we choose to withdraw from a relationship, and especially if this takes place within the environment of the church, you can be sure that someone – some "concerned brother" – is going to come up and "should on you." They will tell you that you have hurt the person you are not associating with and you "should" fix it. They will remind you how we are to love one another. And if you want to turn up the heat even more, just draw some boundaries in your own family and extended family! "But she is your sister! Nothing is more important than family!" Yes, but though she is an earthly, flesh and blood sister, she is not a safe person to be in relationship with and I choose not to have that relationship. That is my right. In fact, it is wisdom.

You have the right to choose your friends. You have the right to choose NOT to have or to continue in a relationship with anyone who is unsafe for you. In fact, you might even say that God instructs us – dare we say, commands us – to avoid such relationships! And I am pretty sure that this means an abuse victim has the right before God to separate from and divorce a wicked, abuser-type spouse. That is a yoke that is good to break. That is freedom.

# 63

# CHURCH LEADERS CHARGE
# *VICTIMS* WITH SIN

*"So I exhort the elders among you, as a fellow elder and a witness of the sufferings of Christ, as well as a partaker in the glory that is going to be revealed: shepherd the flock of God that is among you, exercising oversight, not under compulsion, but willingly, as God would have you; not for shameful gain, but eagerly; not domineering over those in your charge, but being examples to the flock." (1 Pet. 5:1-3)*

*"Obey your leaders and submit to them, for they are keeping watch over your souls, as those who will have to give an account. Let them do this with joy and not with groaning, for that would be of no advantage to you." (Hebrews 13:17)*

HARDLY A WEEK GOES BY that we do not receive a report of a local church – pastor and leaders – threatening to or actually exercising discipline (up to ex-communication) on an abuse victim. Generally, a woman. Why? Because she refuses to reconcile, return to, submit to her abuser. The church tells her God does not permit her to divorce.

And they cite verses like Hebrews 13:17 above, but in language that makes it sound like they are covered regarding Peter's instruction to them not to lord it over the flock. "We are saddened and grieved. We love you and your husband. We want the best for you and your family. It grieves us to tears that you have not obeyed our instruction to return and be reconciled." Yada, yada, yada. Same old schtick. Usually these kinds of letters save the real punch for last – "And unless you do obey, we will be forced to enact church discipline upon you."

So, what about this church authority business?

The local church has indeed been given Christ's authority. For what? *To deal with unrepentant sin in people who claim to be Christians.* The church has the authority to hand such a one over to Satan (see 1 Cor 5) and Christ stands with the church in that action when rightfully carried out. A church that will not obey the Lord in this regard is sinning. Their authority rests *in the Scriptures.*

Now, here's the thing. In these abuse cases (and probably in many others as well) what is happening repeatedly is that THE WICKED PERSON – THE ABUSER – IS NOT BEING PUT OUT OF THE CHURCH, THE VICTIM IS!! Happens all the time. ALL the time! And why is she being put out? Because she will not "obey" the pastor/elders instruction to return to her abuser, remain married, and never divorce.

Alright then. Let's move on a bit further here and ask the pertinent question:

*Does the local church have the authority given by god to grant or deny permission to divorce? or, to put it this way, does a person need to obtain the permission of their church before they can divorce?*

These churches would answer both questions "YES"!

And I am telling them, NO YOU DO NOT.

What churches DO have the authority to deal with is sin in *unrepentant professing Christians* – like abusers. The only authority the church has is the Word of God. And although there are legions of rankly arrogant church leaders around today who insist that *their* take on what the Scriptures say about marriage, divorce, and remarriage is the infallible, inerrant position, what kind of person, really, is going to insist that THEIR position is correct when in fact it is obvious that so many Christians disagree on these subjects? *Yet these people will actually ex-communicate an abuse victim for not submitting to their interpretation and obeying them.*

You do NOT need your church's permission to divorce. Yes, if you sinfully abandon your spouse for selfish, evil reasons, then you are sinning and it is your SIN that the church has authority to deal with. But where – show me chapter and verse – where does the Bible EVER say that the local church has the "keys" that the Pope claims to hold when it comes to granting or denying marital divorce? Where? It isn't in the Bible. It is an invented tradition of man that is holding so many people in bondage.

I have victims contact me regularly, all in fear and terrible anxiety, because they know they are being abused, they know in their own conscience God is leading them to leave their abuser, but their church is overtly or covertly threatening to ex-communicate them from the kingdom of God, and so they don't know what to do. I tell them all the same thing. Don't fear those threats. Laugh at them. They hold no authority over you in your decision to leave your abuser. You do not need the church's permission to divorce.

Pastors, elders, and church members – all of you who keep laying this enslaving false teaching on people – YOU are playing the role of the false teachers the Apostle Paul warns us all against who hinder people from the kingdom of God. Yep, it's YOU:

*"You were running well. Who hindered you from obeying the truth? This persuasion is not from him who calls you." (Galatians 5:7-8)*

No, this persuasion is NOT from the Lord. It is from YOU guys who are lording it over the flock and claiming authority for yourselves that Christ never gave you. You know what He says about you? This –

*"I wish those who unsettle you would emasculate them-selves!" (Galatians 5:12)*

And the Lord also exposes your real motive in treating victims like you do –

> *"It is those who want to make a good showing in the flesh who would force you to be circumcised, and only in order that they may not be persecuted for the cross of Christ."*
> *(Galatians 6:12)*

Oh, I've seen the game. I know the company line. No divorce for abuse. No divorce except for adultery and even if the guy does adulterate, God's best is for you to stay in the game. That's the line. That's the "approved tradition" of the usual culprits who sit on stages at conference after conference (which I gave up attending long ago) and write the books (which I quit buying long ago) and garner the oohs and ahhs from the masses (that I never received). And you, the disciples of these culprits, all know full well that if you stray from their company line, it's going to cost you. So, you just keep perpetuating these perversions of God's Word else you know that you might have to pay up like a creationist professor in a typical evolutionary university. I know. I have seen it over and over again. I have personally communicated with big name church leaders who privately admit that divorce for abuse is right but then say "but if you tell anyone I said that I will deny it." Yep, that's what they say.

You, the victims of abuse or other wrongs that destroy the marriage covenant – you do not need the permission of your pastor, of your elders, of your church to divorce. And when they insist that you do, when they start the rumblings and threatenings of the excommunication machinery, shake your head, knock their dust off your shoes, and move on with no fear into freedom.

# 64

# HOW TO SPOT AN ABUSER WHO
# CLAIMS TO BE THE VICTIM

I AM SURE that you have watched police SWAT teams in action at a hostage situation. As the hostages emerge, a strange thing happens. The police treat them as if they were the bad guys. They have them kneel down, hands in the air, frisk them and handcuff them. Why? Because if the police have never actually seen the suspects, they want to be sure that the bad guys aren't trying to escape in the disguise of one of the hostages. And that is how we need to handle abuse situations, because it is very, very common for the abuser to claim to be the victim – and his disguise can be pretty ingenious. Many hostages are thrown in "jail" while the bad guys go free when it comes to how our churches are dealing with abuse in their midst.

It really is not that difficult to recognize an abuser. Their mentality of power, control, entitlement and justification always betrays itself in their speech and you can hear it if you know what to listen for. To show you what I mean, let me use an example for a not-so-well-disguised abuser who wrote to me recently. He claims to be the victim of his wife's abuse. I will just paraphrase him so as not to publicly identify him. I suppose on a blog like this I have to protect the guilty. Oh well. Here's his opening line:

> *"Too bad you don't really know what you are talking about. You do not have much discernment and have bought into the lie that all or most domestic violence is perpetrated by men against women, nothing could be further from the truth. I can also tell you don't have any personal experience in this area, and I do. You, like many*

*others have bought into the lies about DV and you say it's mostly women who have come forward to you, therefore it must be only or mostly women that are abused."*

And then:

*"She lies, deceives, manipulates and much of what you say of what happens spiritually is true, but I am the Christian and she unfortunately is not, I suggest her Catholic upbringing may have something to do with that. Her family are liars and deceivers...she would come to you and say how I beat her, the kids, control the money and more...and you would believe it...like her family and few friends...but most neighbors, our children and their friends know the truth."*

So, when you are confronted with a man who claims to be the victim, here are some pretty reliable tests you can apply to see if you are talking to a real victim, or an abuser who is playing the victim (thus attempting to win you over as his ally) –

- Abusers evidence a mentality of superiority and certainty. Notice how this fellow goes right on the attack to exalt himself, his knowledge, his wisdom as oppose to our ignorance. He knows. We are fools. In contrast, a real victim is most often confused, uncertain, and has a low self-image, putting themselves down.

- Abusers will evidence a demeaning attitude toward women in general and their victim in particular. They insist that radical feminism has us all duped and that they are the victims of some widespread anti-man conspiracy. Victims don't see things this clearly and thus are not so dogmatic. They will be more demeaning of themselves if anything.

- Abusers attack their victim with nasty, cruel allegations. For example, the abuser may say "My wife is a drunk, a whore, a lazy *^%$ who only thinks of herself and lies to everyone about me."

We need to ask ourselves, is what this guy is saying about his wife really believable? Often the abuser's accusations are bizarre and outlandish. Real victims do not exaggerate their abuser's conduct; rather, they tend to downplay or not report all the evil things the abuser has done because they are trying to not tell lies and because they may have suppressed memories of abusive incidents while trying to walk on eggshells and survive.

If a victim may has come to the point of realizing the evils the abuser has done, the victim may report the abuse to others to seek help and support, but the victim won't exaggerate and invent lies like the abuser does.

Abuse victims, and perhaps especially genuine male victims of abuse, exhibit humility and shame. They are far more reluctant to open up about what has happened to them. They will not insist that they have lots of people who believe them! Real abuse victims, you see, often lack allies. It is the abuser who has them!

# 65

# MARRIAGE, VOWS AND DIVORCE

The following is an excerpt from my book, *A Cry for Justice*:

<u>What about those promises made at the wedding?</u>

> *"Let what you say be simply 'Yes' or 'No'; anything more than this comes from evil." (Matthew 5:37)*

<u>Contracts</u>

YOU ARE PROBABLY BOUND to more of them than you might realize. Credit cards come with them. You finance your car, buy a home with a mortgage, and enter into an employment agreement with your boss. All of these aspects of normal life involve contracts. And they all have sanctions. Blessings or curses, we might say. If I buy a new flat screen TV with my credit card, I am promising to pay the debt off in a particular time, with a specified interest rate, and if I do so, I will be blessed. I get to keep the TV. If not, well, the curses go into play! Some burly repo man might show up at my door, or my paycheck could be slapped with a garnishment.

For a number of years, I have wondered about one of the most important contracts human beings make. It is the marriage contract, entered into (we even use those words "entered into" at the wedding!) with vows recited in the presence of God and witnesses. My confusion about these vows originates in the fact that for the most part, the church tells people their marriage contract is non-enforceable. This is particularly evident when we consider abuse and the marriage vows. Consider a typical vow:

- To love.

- To honor.

- To cherish.

- To forsake all others.

- Until death.

Normally, at least in a Christian ceremony, these vows are expressly stated to be made "solemnly," in the sight of God, and witnessed by everyone present. And yet, *unlike every other human contract in life*, it seems that this contract can be disregarded the first day after the honeymoon with full immunity from sanctions (curses) and continued enjoyment of all privilege. Isn't, as we say, something really wrong with this picture? A spouse can, for example, never love, never honor, never cherish their wife or husband, and yet we tell the wronged party that there is nothing to be done about it. They are married, the contract is binding, and that is that. Perhaps if there is adultery, then yes, divorce is permitted. Otherwise, the defrauded party is still bound by contract. What? Say that again?

Marriage is a contract. That may not sound very romantic, but contract is the essence of the wedding ceremony, and the vows are the means by which husband and wife enter into this contract (see Proverbs 2:17; Malachi 2:14). Each one of them states the terms, the blessings for keeping their "part of the bargain," and the curses for breaking the deal. Essentially, the curse comes from the fact that the vows are recited in "the presence of God and these witnesses," acknowledging that, as the London Confession of Faith states, God is being invoked to either bless or curse us. In that respect, wedding vows are made to God!

*"A lawful oath is a part of religious worship, wherein the person swearing in truth, righteousness, and judgment, solemnly calls God to witness what he swears, and to judge him according to the truth or falseness thereof....*

*Whoever takes an oath warranted by the Word of God, ought duly to consider the weightiness of so solemn an act, and therein to vow nothing but what he knows to be truth; because by rash, false, and vain oaths, the Lord is provoked, and for them this land mourns." [Chapter 23, The London Confession of Faith, modern language].*

Today, people often want to write their own vows for their wedding. If I am the officiating minister, I discourage this or at least reserve the right to review what they propose. Why? Because I recognize that vows are to be more than mere flowery, vapory, feel-good words that evaporate as they are uttered. But the vows are the terms of the contract, entered into before God. As such, they are solemn. While a wedding is indeed cause for celebration, I wonder how the atmosphere of many "party-on" ceremonies would be radically changed to a more sober sense if everyone realized just what was actually happening? "Lord, we call upon you to bless us or curse us according to the vows we are now making." Perhaps some marriages wouldn't even take place! Perhaps the realization of this is what prompted the disciples to ask Jesus:

*"The disciples said to him, 'If such is the case of a man with his wife, it is better not to marry.'" (Matthew 19:10)*

Once we recognize that marriage is a contract, entered into with sober vows, we are in a position to define divorce – something that is often overlooked in many treatments of this subject. What we mean by "divorce" is not always as clear as we think. *Divorce is the breaking of the marriage contract.* It is effecting separation of what God has joined together by violation of the vows, the terms of the deal. Therefore:

- Divorce, or the effecting of the "separation" that Jesus forbids (see Matthew 19:6; Mark 10:9), is committed by the <u>guilty</u> party; by the marriage partner who actually breaks the contract.

- Divorce is *never* effected by the innocent partner. In fact, it is *impossible* for the innocent partner to effect a divorce.

- When the wronged spouse takes the legal means to end the marriage (i.e., files for divorce with the civil authorities) he or she *is not divorcing, but is merely acknowledging the divorce that has already taken place.*

What Jesus forbids, in other words, when He says, "What therefore God has joined together, let not man separate," *is the destruction of the marriage by violation of the vows.* That is what divorce is. Divorce, we say again, is <u>not</u> the filing of the paperwork by the wronged party.

Some years ago, when I was counseling a couple whose background included a history of adultery by one of them, I remember telling them, "Your marriage is over. It was destroyed by the violation of the marriage contract you made. Therefore, the wronged party has the right to acknowledge this fact by filing the necessary legal papers with the civil court. You are not required to do so. You may choose to forgive and continue in the marriage. But this is your right." In this case, the wronged spouse chose to forgive and continue. Perhaps in cases like this it would be appropriate to recite new vows?

In the case of abuse in marriage: *the abuse victim is not the one "committing" the divorce when he or she decides the marriage contract has been rendered null and void.* That has already been accomplished by the abuser who has refused to love, honor, and cherish as he vowed before God to do. The church continues, in many cases, to do great harm and injustice to abuse victims when we insist that if she files for divorce, she is actually the one who is effecting the divorce and therefore, guilty before God. All the victim is doing is *suing* for the court to recognize that the marriage contract has been broken. We even use that legal language – suing for divorce.

*Why is it that we seem to hold credit card agreements and home mortgages in higher esteem than the marriage contract? What person in their right mind would ever enter into a contract, knowing that the other party can violate the terms to our harm, and yet there will be nothing we can do to get out of the contract?*

# THE CASE AGAINST THE "PERMANENCE VIEW"

*"And to the angel of the church in Laodicea write: 'The words of the Amen, the faithful and true witness, the beginning of God's creation. 'I know your works: you are neither cold nor hot. Would that you were either cold or hot! So, because you are lukewarm, and neither hot nor cold, I will spit you out of my mouth.'" (Revelation 3:14-16)*

I SUPPOSE THAT our Lord's words here to the lukewarm church at Laodicea could possibly not mean that He would reject them forever if they did not repent, but "spitting out" of His mouth does tend to lead us to that conclusion.  Similarly, His warning that He would remove the lampstand of the Ephesian church out of its place if they did not repent sounds rather final as well.

But here is my point.  There are numbers of Scriptures in the New Testament which indicate that Christ does indeed divorce His "bride" when that bride turns out to be unbelieving, disobedient, and false.  This all runs quite counter of course to the teachings of people like John Piper who claim that divorce is never permissible and argue from the model of Christ and His church.  Consider however:

*"But a man named Ananias, with his wife Sapphira, sold a piece of property, and with his wife's knowledge he kept back for himself some of the proceeds and brought only a part of it and laid it at the apostles' feet. But Peter said, 'Ananias, why has Satan filled your heart to lie to the Holy Spirit and to keep back for yourself part of the proceeds of the land? While it remained unsold, did it not remain your*

*own? And after it was sold, was it not at your disposal?
Why is it that you have contrived this deed in your heart?
You have not lied to men but to God.' When Ananias heard
these words, he fell down and breathed his last. And great
fear came upon all who heard of it." (Acts 5:1-5)*

I suspect some people would try to argue that Ananias and his
wife Sapphira were actually genuine believers and this business of
striking them dead was just a form of discipline from their
heavenly Father. I don't think so. I think this was a public
exposure of false brethren. A rather final divorce. Here is another
divorce of professing Christians:

*"But now I am writing to you not to associate with anyone
who bears the name of brother if he is guilty of sexual
immorality or greed, or is an idolater, reviler, drunkard,
or swindler – not even to eat with such a one. For
what have I to do with judging outsiders? Is it not those
inside the church whom you are to judge? God judges
those outside. 'Purge the evil person from among you.'"
(1 Corinthians 5:11-13)*

And again:

*"For certain people have crept in unnoticed who long ago
were designated for this condemnation, ungodly people,
who pervert the grace of our God into sensuality and deny
our only Master and Lord, Jesus Christ." (Jude 1:4)*

These "hidden reefs" as Jude calls them a bit later obviously
profess to be Christians. That is how they "creep in." Jude says
that the Lord will judge them. Once again, Christ divorces a false,
unfaithful bride. He disciplines and purifies His true people and
will never let them go. But as He dealt with Israel in the Old
Testament, so the author of Hebrews tells us He deals with those
who profess His name today:

*"Therefore we must pay much closer attention to what we have heard, lest we drift away from it. For since the message declared by angels proved to be reliable, and every transgression or disobedience received a just retribution, how shall we escape if we neglect such a great salvation? It was declared at first by the Lord, and it was attested to us by those who heard..." (Hebrews 2:1-3)*

And once more:

*"Therefore, as the Holy Spirit says, 'Today, if you hear his voice, do not harden your hearts as in the rebellion, on the day of testing in the wilderness, where your fathers put me to the test and saw my works for forty years. Therefore I was provoked with that generation, and said, 'They always go astray in their heart; they have not known my ways.' As I swore in my wrath, 'They shall not enter my rest.' Take care, brothers, lest there be in any of you an evil, unbelieving heart, leading you to fall away from the living God. But exhort one another every day, as long as it is called 'today,' that none of you may be hardened by the deceitfulness of sin. For we have come to share in Christ, if indeed we hold our original confidence firm to the end.*

*As it is said, 'Today, if you hear his voice, do not harden your hearts as in the rebellion.' For who were those who heard and yet rebelled? Was it not all those who left Egypt led by Moses? And with whom was he provoked for forty years? Was it not with those who sinned, whose bodies fell in the wilderness? And to whom did he swear that they would not enter his rest, but to those who were disobedient? So we see that they were unable to enter because of unbelief." (Hebrews 3:7-19)*

Hebrews clearly connects the experience of these false Israelites in the Old Testament with our experience in the New Testament era. Anyone who hears Christ's voice and bears the name Christian, but in the end hardens his heart and is unbelieving and disobedient, will never enter heaven. Christ will reject them. He will, I would say, divorce them.

One more time:

> *"Not everyone who says to me, 'Lord, Lord,' will enter the kingdom of heaven, but the one who does the will of my Father who is in heaven. On that day many will say to me, 'Lord, Lord, did we not prophesy in your name, and cast out demons in your name, and do many mighty works in your name?' And then will I declare to them, 'I never knew you; depart from me, you workers of lawlessness.'"* (Matthew 7:21-23)

Therefore, when a Christian finds themselves married to an abuser, and even (perhaps especially) when that abuser claims to be a Christian, how is it not Christlike to divorce that abuser? How is remaining in such a "marriage" a model of how Christ deals with people who claim to belong to Him but in fact do not? Not even the true, genuine local church is to allow such a person to remain in its ranks but is to put them out. To divorce them, we could even say.

"Depart from me, you workers of lawlessness." The words of the Lord Jesus Himself.

# 67

# WHAT IT MEANS TO HAVE NO CONSCIENCE

*"Blessed is the man against whom the LORD counts no iniquity, and in whose spirit there is no deceit. For when I kept silent, my bones wasted away through my groaning all day long. For day and night your hand was heavy upon me; my strength was dried up as by the heat of summer. Selah. I acknowledged my sin to you, and I did not cover my iniquity; I said, 'I will confess my transgressions to the LORD,' and you forgave the iniquity of my sin. Selah."*
*(Psalm 32:2-5)*

THE HUMAN CONSCIENCE is a powerful thing. It is a powerful thing in the life of the Christian. As David found out when he sinned, the Lord uses our conscience to put a heavy hand upon us when we sin. So intense is the Lord's working through our conscience that under His conviction we are without strength, dried up, like a man lost in the heat of the desert. The only remedy is genuine repentance and confession of sin, and then God's forgiveness. Notice then that the truly repentant person can *feel* that forgiveness, in contrast to the heavy misery of a convicted conscience.

This is a powerful truth to hold onto when you come under temptation. Sin tells us that we can indulge ourselves and enjoy it. But the fact is, as David and myriads of Christians have found, when a Christian yields and sins, if there is any enjoyment at all it is over in seconds. Then comes that terrible heat of conscience. The heavy hand of the Lord driving us to confession and repentance. It is a miserable thing. Day and night. Day and night. You wake up at 3AM with a knot in your gut and your sin right before you. You cannot concentrate. You have done wrong and you know and feel that wrongness. So don't be duped by temptation. If you are a real Christian, you cannot enjoy sin. It just won't work.

Now, as most all of you know, the person we call an abuser has little or no conscience. He can play the holy saint outwardly, then all the while inwardly and out of sight he lives in wickedness. Think about this. He has no conscience, or a seared conscience (they are pretty much the same thing). If you have ever felt the intensity of misery that a violated conscience can bring, then just mull over the fact that the abuser can do what he does – abuse – and experience no pangs of conscience. He can sleep at night. In fact, he even delights in his evil. He feeds on it. It is sweet to him.

Think about this. Dwell on it. The thing is incredible. It shows us the degree of the evil we are dealing with in this abuse thing. Here is a person who can do incredible wickedness against his own wife (*who has hated his own flesh?* as Paul says), and not only does it not bother him, but when he sees her suffering, he rejoices in it. He is energized by it.

Do you understand? Most professing Christians and pastors do not. This is evil. These are the evil people who most certainly are in this world. If we fail to understand the depth of their wickedness, the conscienceless nature of their minds, and if we instead assume they are like us, then we are going to go miserably wrong and we will be duped by them. We will think we can fix them. We will feel sorry for them. But Scripture tells us their true nature:

> *"But these people, like irrational animals – creatures of instinct born to be caught and destroyed – speak blasphemies about things they don't understand, and in their destruction they too will be destroyed, suffering harm as the payment for unrighteousness. They consider it a pleasure to carouse in the daytime. They are spots and*

*blemishes, delighting in their deceptions as they feast with you. They have eyes full of adultery and are always looking for sin. They seduce unstable people and have hearts trained in greed." (2 Peter 2:12-14a)*

So, we must know what we are dealing with. We must believe what God's Word tells us about the reality of evil around us and particularly as it creeps in amongst us in the local church.

And largely, "we" (the visible, professing Christian church), do not.

# 68

# DEBATING BIBLE WITH AN ABUSER IS A WASTE OF TIME

*"And when he entered the temple, the chief priests and the elders of the people came up to him as he was teaching, and said, 'By what authority are you doing these things, and who gave you this authority?' Jesus answered them, 'I also will ask you one question, and if you tell me the answer, then I also will tell you by what authority I do these things. The baptism of John, from where did it come? From heaven or from man?' And they discussed it among themselves, saying, 'If we say, 'From heaven,' he will say to us, 'Why then did you not believe him?' But if we say, 'From man,' we are afraid of the crowd, for they all hold that John was a prophet.' So they answered Jesus, 'We do not know.' And he said to them, 'Neither will I tell you by what authority I do these things.'" (Matthew 21:23-27)*

NO ONE EVER WON a debate with Jesus. Imagine, arguing a point from God's Word with God! Now there is a formula for being made to look like a real idiot. Which is, of course, what happened to the scribes and Pharisees and anyone else who thought they could trip Him up.

Much like the Pharisees, the abusive person who pretends to be a Christian loves to quote Scripture to his victim. Then he asks them questions about it. "Huh, huh, come on, come on …isn't that right?" It is my opinion that it is a waste of time to get drawn in by such a tactic, and you certainly will never convince him anyway.

Notice what Jesus did in the case above. He had a question all ready for them. I like that. "I will answer your question about the Bible telling a wife to submit to her husband, if you first answer this question for me." Then put the question to him – "God says that anyone who claims to love Him but hates their brother (or wife) is a liar. Tell me why, from the way you treat me, I should conclude that you are a Christian."

One time I met a pastor in his office to confront him with being abusive to his congregation. He told me that unless I could open up my Bible and show him that God's Word says what he had done is sin, then he didn't have to listen to me. I told him I wasn't going to do that (I had my Bible there). He snickered, not too subtly indicating that I was no match for him in a Bible debate. But I told him I wasn't going to quote him chapter and verse because it would do no good. If he wasn't ready to hear a fellow pastor who had known him for some time, then no amount of Bible verses would mean anything to him either.

Abusers use Scripture to attack their victim. They use Bible talk to mask their own evil. Jesus had a way of stripping that disguise right off and getting down to the real issue – the evil motive and heart of His enemy. I suggest we do the same.

# 69

# The Fundamental Motivation
## of the Abuser

*"For this is the message that you have heard from the beginning, that we should love one another. We should not be like Cain, who was of the evil one and murdered his brother. And why did he murder him? Because his own deeds were evil and his brother's righteous. Do not be surprised, brothers, that the world hates you. We know that we have passed out of death into life, because we love the brothers. Whoever does not love abides in death. (1 John 3:11-14)*

I BELIEVE I HAVE WRITTEN before on these verses, particularly on verse 12, but I am compelled to write again.

This phrase is familiar to most all of you – *"Why Does He do That?"* – as it is the main title of Lundy Bancroft's wonderful and foundational book that has helped so many people learn what they could not learn in their churches.[14] Namely, abusers abuse because they have a profound mentality of entitlement to power and control and feel fully justified in using whatever tactics they must to obtain and maintain that self-deifying power.

But let me suggest that Scripture tells us there is perhaps an even more basic answer to the question, "Why does he do that?" And it is this –

---

[14] As always when I mention Bancroft, I want to caution you not to take your theology from him. His Why Does He do That? book is a very excellent tool. But Lundy has some very, very strange ideas about religion.

*The wicked hate the righteous with a murderous hatred simply because their own deeds are evil and their victims are righteous.*

Darkness despises light because the light exposes what the darkness hides. Light breaks the power of darkness.

The liar despises the truth because the truth robs the liar of his deceiving power over others. Liars hate the truth because they are liars and the truth is truth.

The world hates Jesus Christ because the world is antichrist, and Christ is King of kings.

You see it here in the words of the Psalmist —

*"Why do the nations rage and the peoples plot in vain? The kings of the earth set themselves, and the rulers take counsel together, against the LORD and against his Anointed, saying, 'Let us burst their bonds apart and cast away their cords from us.'" (Psalm 2:1-3)*

Why do the nations rage? Because the Lord is the Lord and they are not.

I have absolutely no doubt that the murderous, destructive hatred of the abuser (especially the kind of abuser who claims to be a Christian) rages against his victim simply because she is righteous, and he is evil. In the world today, even in and perhaps especially in the West, domestic violence and abuse are perhaps THE leading form of persecution against Christians.

Listen to it once more —

*"We should not be like Cain, who was of the evil one and murdered his brother. And why did he murder him? Because his own deeds were evil and his brother's righteous." (1 John 3:12)*

Understand? Why does your abuser abuse and hate you? Why? Because he is evil. Because you are not.

And it really requires coming to grips with all of this in order to begin to see the blinding, deceptive, fog cast by the abuser begin to fade and lift. He is evil. Not difficult. Evil. Not damaged by his childhood. Evil. And no matter how skillfully he constructs a disguise of holiness, inside there is a wicked, evil heart that hates all good.

*"We know that we have passed out of death into life, because we love the brothers. Whoever does not love abides in death."*

# 70

# ABUSERS OFTEN DO THEIR EVIL "BEHIND THE SCENES"

*"If we say we have fellowship with him while we walk in darkness, we lie and do not practice the truth." (1 John 1:6)*

ABUSERS ARE DARKNESS. Sin is darkness. Abusers live and think and exist and operate in the kingdom of darkness under the rule of their god, the Prince of Darkness. They have tactics that are a devilish version of Frodo's elvish cloak that could conceal him. While an abuser may, at times, accuse and mind-game his victim publicly (though even then in a way that provides him with plausible deniability), he quite often operates behind this cloak, in the darkness, out of the sight of others. He isolates, then he strikes.

It took me years of hard knocks to get this through my head. "Pastor, can we just talk? Just you and me?" Warning! Warning! Look out. Don't do it. But of course, Jeff often went right ahead and took the bait. We neurotics have that conscience you know that is so easily bothered. The abuser knows that full well.

My experience with the wicked during my years as a pastor has been very, very similar and usually even identical, to the trials you all have been through at the hands of your abuser. So, I know that what happened to me has happened to most all of you. Abusers will frequently isolate through deception, then strike.

People have come to me over the years and asked to talk to me about a "concern." Now, I have been burned so many times following that kind of request that I must admit my defenses quickly go up, unless of course it is someone that I know loves me and whom I can trust. But, you know, as a pastor we are supposed to be open and transparent and vulnerable and.... right? Wrong! We are supposed to be wise as serpents and innocent (of evil ourselves) as doves. There is a big difference. You all have found that out yourselves after being set up for an attack so many, many times. So, here comes a wicked person. His tactic is to accuse, and this time to accuse in a way that really plays with your mind and plants false guilt and self-doubt. He wants to speak to you alone. "Can we just, talk?" "We don't need to involve anyone else in this." "Just you and me. Like Matthew 18 you know." So, you sit down and let him begin. After all, maybe he has a valid point?

Of course, by now Jeff should know full well that it's a set up. But aren't we supposed to be patient and longsuffering with a Christian brother? So you listen. No one else there. Just you and him. Then, here come the accusations. "Jeff, YOU are (select one), unkind/hard to talk to/bitter/unforgiving/not called to be a pastor....and on and on it can go.

Now I have seen something very interesting in these cases. Of course, it took me decades to get to the point of recognizing what was going on and calling such a person on their evil. If you stop the conversation when the accusations start spewing and say something like, 'we need to have witnesses here so that they too can hear your "concerns," the evil one begins to squirm. Now, he may get angry and bullying in some cases. But he will almost always insist, "No! This is between you and me! We don't need anyone else involved." This is all completely contrary to the instruction of Scripture:

> *"Do not admit a charge against an elder except on the evidence of two or three witnesses. As for those who persist in sin, rebuke them in the presence of all, so that the rest may stand in fear." (1 Timothy 5:19-20)*

In some cases, in which this has happened to me, when I have insisted on witnesses, hell itself breaks forth in fury. I have seen such evil ones literally thrash around in their chair, going into almost a delirium and behaving and talking as if the very end of the world had come. "You have totally destroyed any good that would come of this meeting! You just HAD to involve others!" Thrash some more. Throw arms around more. Jump up and pace around the room. Throw self back down in the chair again and thrash around some more. Really. Honest. It happened.

Or I have had the reaction to my insistence upon witnesses be one of mocking. "Now, Pastor, you know full well that what I am saying is truth. You know you are guilty." All of this said with an evil smirk on the face.

You understand, right? These kinds that I am describing are not mere "difficult" members of the flock who we must be extra patient with. Mere people who are hard to communicate with. Or people with troubled histories, victims of their own past. No! This is evil and darkness in action. These are children of the evil one. That is how the Lord Jesus called it. "You are of your father the devil. He was a murderer from the beginning. He is the father of lies." And so are his children.

I cannot imagine (well, to some degree I can) what it would be like to be MARRIED to one of these, having to dwell under the same roof and share the same bed. My suffering at the hands of the wicked has been nothing compared to what most of you have suffered. The abuser has you alone most anytime he wants to. And that aloneness is a kind of darkness which allows him to work his evil enchantments. This is one of the most powerful reasons we here at Unholy Charade realize that *a marriage to an abuser does not need to be fixed. It needs to be ended.* And the true Church of the Lord Jesus Christ will help the victim end it, not insist that she remain a prisoner in that psychological torture chamber set of fire by hell itself.

*"Now when Sanballat and Tobiah and Geshem the Arab and the rest of our enemies heard that I had built the wall and that there was no breach left in it (although up to that time I had not set up the doors in the gates), Sanballat and Geshem sent to me, saying, 'Come and let us meet together at Hakkephirim in the plain of Ono.' But they intended to*

*do me harm. And I sent messengers to them, saying, 'I am doing a great work and I cannot come down. Why should the work stop while I leave it and come down to you?'"*
*(Nehemiah 6:1-3)*

# 71

# An Arrogant Church
# Enables the Wicked

*"Some are arrogant, as though I were not coming to you."*
*(1Corinthians 4:18)*

*"It is actually reported that there is sexual immorality among you, and of a kind that is not tolerated even among pagans, for a man has his father's wife. And you are arrogant! Ought you not rather to mourn? Let him who has done this be removed from among you. For though absent in body, I am present in spirit; and as if present, I have already pronounced judgment on the one who did such a thing. When you are assembled in the name of the Lord Jesus and my spirit is present, with the power of our Lord Jesus, you are to deliver this man to Satan for the destruction of the flesh, so that his spirit may be saved in the day of the Lord. Your boasting is not good...."*
*(1Corinthians 5:1-6a)*

WE HAVE OFTEN WRITTEN on the topic of local churches enabling abusers, allowing them to remain in the church, even allowing them in many cases to be members in "good standing," while – you all know the familiar scenario – the victim of the abuser is guilted, dismissed, or even ex-communicated. And we have often discussed why this happens. How can it be? I believe the Apostle Paul gives us the answer in the verses cited above, at least the answer in a good many cases – arrogance.

Look what Paul says to these Corinthians. He is shocked. They are permitting a grossly evil man to remain among them, no doubt counting him as a brother in Christ. This was no small sin. His fornication was of a startling nature, so much so that not even the pagan world would permit it. And you are arrogant. There it is. They should have mourned and been grieved that such a terrible sin was in their midst. But they didn't. They boasted. I suppose they boasted about the grace of God and about how gracious they were in not being judgmental. Same old shtick we hear today so often.

Now, I want to tweak this Scripture just a bit. I think it's ok with the Lord. Here goes:

*It is actually reported that there is domestic abuse among you, and of a kind that is not tolerated even among pagans, for a man is cruelly abusing his wife while he claims to follow Christ. And you are arrogant! Ought you not rather to mourn? Let him who has done this be removed from among you. For though absent in body, I am present in spirit; and as if present, I have already pronounced judgment on the one who did such a thing. When you are assembled in the name of the Lord Jesus and my spirit is present, with the power of our Lord Jesus, you are to deliver this man to Satan for the destruction of the flesh, so that his spirit may be saved in the day of the Lord. Your boasting is not good...*

You say that you want to "help" this wicked man? Then do what the Apostle says. Put him out of the church. Deliver this abuser over to Satan not only to protect the church from thinking this evil is permissible, but also so that Satan can have at him and maybe, just MAYBE, he will repent and his spirit be saved when Christ returns.[15] THAT is God's prescribed therapy for the abuser.

---

[15] Pastor Sam Powell believes that the "spirit" to be saved is actually the spirit or Spirit in, the church. In this case Paul is not saying that the wicked man might repent and be saved, but that it is the church that needs to be protected. I think you can find Sam's article on his My Only Comfort blog. For myself, I do not believe that abusers who have played the hypocrite for years and who are abusers as we define them here, ever repent.

Don't keep him in the church. Don't get him into some kind of therapy program to cure his anger. Don't "love on him" until he is overwhelmed with warm fuzzies and repents. Put him out! Pronounce him cut off from Christ. Put him out into the world that he wants to be like and let Satan have at him.

All of this of course will require some serious humbling. That spirit of arrogance must be confessed and rejected. Heads need to hang low and tears of repentance need to be shed, then action in keeping with that repentance must be taken. Put the man out.

What is wrong in our churches today? Why is this abuse hiding in the pulpits a virtual plague? And why won't pastors and church leaders, for the most part – or church members – listen when we try to tell them what is going on among them? Why do so few pastors come to training seminars on domestic violence? Why? I am convinced Paul would tell us the answer in these words:

*"And you are arrogant."*

# 72

# Are You Finding Rest
# for Your Soul?

*"Come to me, all who labor and are heavy laden, and I will give you rest. Take my yoke upon you, and learn from me, for I am gentle and lowly in heart, and you will find rest for your souls. For my yoke is easy, and my burden is light." (Matthew 11:28-30)*

As most all of you know, the reports we receive from oppressed victims of abusers is not this: "I went to my church for help and they were incredible. They helped me get free from this bondage of abuse." Sometimes, every once in a while, we do get such a report and the Lord certainly blesses a church like that. But the norm is quite the opposite. The yoke put upon victims is anything but easy and light. Gentleness and humility are not the typical qualities victims find in their churches.

This is not Jesus Christ.

All through Scripture from Genesis to Revelation we have accounts of false shepherds who lay heavy burdens on the Lord's people. We are warned against them and instructed not to yield to them for a moment. For example:

*"Then Jesus said to the crowds and to his disciples, 'The scribes and the Pharisees sit on Moses' seat, so practice and observe whatever they tell you–but not what they do. For they preach, but do not practice. They tie up heavy burdens, hard to bear, and lay them on people's shoulders, but they themselves are not willing to move them with their finger.'" (Matthew 23:1-4)*

And of course many of the New Testament Epistles such as 2 Corinthians, Galatians, 2 Peter, Jude and others were written because false teachers with a false gospel were coming in among the churches and putting the people back into bondage to some kind of works righteousness. They did not represent Jesus Christ.

Many of us have grown up in the church. And sadly, many of us have been weaned on man's traditions parading as the Word of God. Inevitably those traditions are either rank libertinism (sin all you want because we are under grace) or just as commonly, legalism. It takes Christians raised in such settings a long time to get out from under the load of such a yoke, and many abuse victims have remained in bondage to abuse for many years because they had this yoke of false, man-made teachings laid upon them all their lives.

How can we sort it all out? Well, Christ's words above are a huge help. The fact is, if the Christianity that you embrace is not giving "rest to your soul," then something is wrong. "No, you cannot divorce your abuser! God does not permit it. Go home and try harder and pray for your husband." I submit to you that this is not Jesus Christ. Christ's words to His people are green pastures and still waters. He leads us into peaceful places where we can rest. Jesus Christ the Good Shepherd restores our souls. Is your soul being restored and are you finding rest in the words you are hearing preached to you? If so, that is wonderful. But if not, they are not the words of our Lord.

> *"A Psalm of David. The LORD is my shepherd; I shall not want. He makes me lie down in green pastures. He leads me beside still waters. He restores my soul. He leads me in paths of righteousness for his name's sake. Even though I walk through the valley of the shadow of death, I will fear no evil, for you are with me; your rod and your staff, they comfort me. You prepare a table before me in the presence of my enemies; you anoint my head with oil; my cup overflows.*

*Surely goodness and mercy shall follow me all the days of my life, and I shall dwell in the house of the LORD forever." (Psalm 23:1-6)*

# 73

# CHASING DOWN THE DRAGON
# NAMED SHAME

*"Do not be conformed to this world, but be transformed by the renewal of your mind, that by testing you may discern what is the will of God, what is good and acceptable and perfect." (Romans 12:2)*

SHAME CAN KEEP A HUMAN BEING enslaved for a lifetime if it is not rooted out, seen for what it is, and conquered. Shame is like an interior parasite, unseen, yet sucking the life out of us. It manifests itself in us with a variety of symptoms, but as with any illness, we must treat the source and not just the symptom.

Here, I just want to record some of the more notable quotes I am coming across as I continue to read about shame. These come from the book *Facing Shame*, by Fossum and Mason:[16]

"Our definition of shame refers to humiliation so painful, embarrassment so deep, and a sense of being so completely diminished that one feels he or she will disappear into a pile of ashes. Shame involves the entire self and self-worth of a human being."

"Shame is an inner sense of being completely diminished or insufficient as a person. It is the self-judging the self. A moment of shame may be humiliation so painful or an indignity so profound that one feels one has been robbed of her or his dignity or exposed as basically inadequate, bad, or worthy of rejection. A pervasive sense of shame is

---

[16] Facing Shame, W.W. Norton and Company, 1989

the ongoing premise that one is fundamentally bad, inadequate, defective, unworthy, or not fully valid as a human being."

"We distinguish between the terms 'guilt' and 'shame.' Guilt is the developmentally more mature, though painful, feeling of regret one has about behavior that has violated a personal value. Guilt does not reflect directly upon one's identity nor diminish one's sense of personal worth. It emanates from an integrated conscience and set of values ... Shame is a painful feeling about oneself as a person ... The roots of shame are in abuse, personal violations, seductions and assaults where one's sense of self has been trampled, one's boundaries defiled."

"A shame-bound family is a family with a self-sustaining, multigenerational system of interaction with a cast of characters who are (or were in their lifetime) loyal to a set of rules and injunctions demanding control, perfectionism, blame and denial. The pattern inhibits or defeats the development of authentic intimate relationships, promotes secrets and vague personal boundaries, unconsciously instills shame in the family members, as well as chaos in their lives, and binds them to perpetuate the shame in themselves and their kin. It does so regardless of the good intentions, wishes, and love which may also be part of the system."

Christ, of course is the real Healer of shame. He has come that we might have abundant life, and of His sheep He says that He is not ashamed to own us as His own. Now we need to get hold of what that really means.

# 74

# Don't be Duped by the Nice One

*"What do you think? A man had two sons. And he went to the first and said, 'Son, go and work in the vineyard today.' And he answered, 'I will not,' but afterward he changed his mind and went. And he went to the other son and said the same. And he answered, 'I go, sir,' but did not go. Which of the two did the will of his father?' They said, 'The first.' Jesus said to them, 'Truly, I say to you, the tax collectors and the prostitutes go into the kingdom of God before you.'" (Matthew 21:28-31)*

I HAVE HAD EXPERIENCE with a number of what I suppose psychologists like Dr George Simon would call the covert-aggressive personality. That is what we have here in this parable. One brother overtly and openly refuses to do his father's bidding. "What a jerk!" we would say as we write him off as a wicked son. But then, he turns around and does it!

Then you have this other brother. You know, the nice one. As soon as dad asks him to go work in the vineyard he is compliant. "You bet!" But then he doesn't do it. His rebellion is covert, hidden, unseen. We think him the nice guy, the wonderful son, the fellow ready and willing to obey. But in reality he is wicked. The niceness is a facade. He has no intention at all of doing what his father asked, though he mouths the words and smiles the smile that makes him look obedient. We like him. He's nice.

Wrong. He is a liar. He has an evil heart given to deception. He is hard and without conscience. And he is more dangerous by far than the open, overt aggressor.

I have known these covert-aggressives. I have told myself and others that I like them in spite of their failures. But I am done fooling myself about them and I am done being fooled. I am finished with liking them. I now see behind the niceness, the smiles, the quick willingness to do whatever they are asked, and I see the wickedness that lurks there. I see a person who not only has no intention of doing what they say, but who, behind that smile, is a liar and a deceiver and a person who cares nothing for me. This is rank aggression. It is abuse.

And perhaps it is a worse form of abuse than that which is openly and plainly hostile.

# 75

# Getting Free of the Bondage of Magical Thinking

*"And when you pray, do not heap up empty phrases as the Gentiles do, for they think that they will be heard for their many words. Do not be like them, for your Father knows what you need before you ask him." (Matthew 6:7-8)*

CHILDREN OFTEN THINK MAGICALLY. They believe that their thoughts or actions or words have the power to cause things to happen, or to not happen. "I wish you were dead!" can later cause the child who uttered it to be in genuine fear that his wish may well become God's command to strike down the sibling he was fighting with earlier. Those of you more knowledgeable than I about psychology could probably have stories to tell about this. I do know that this kind of thing can cause tremendous anxiety to a child who lives in a dysfunctional or abusive home. He is made to feel as if he is the cause of the trouble, and he believes it. Then, he may set out to be sure that he behaves in such a way that insures the trouble never happen again. Of course, the trouble comes anyway – but the child will chalk that up to his own failure.

God is good! I mean, really, really good. His goodness far exceeds our thoughts. And one of the very good things that God does is to refuse to be manipulated by us. Our thoughts, our sins, our good deeds, the intensity and length (or lack thereof) of our prayers or offerings – do not put Him in our debt one cent. God is not obligated. God is free. When God chooses to answer our prayers (which He is most willing to do in Christ), He does so solely out of His goodness, His kindness, and His grace. If our prayers need to be "tweaked" (and they usually do), the Spirit of God intercedes for us (Romans 8).

Nothing – and I mean absolutely nothing – that we do or fail to do can manipulate God. Thus, Christianity is not magical, while I think it could be said that every other religion is. The pagan temples, sacrifices, the priesthood, the cutting of fanatic followers – what are these if not things designed to magically cause some force to act? But the Living and True God is not like that. Not at all. He is not the creation of man's imagination, and He cannot be tamed to do our bidding.

What has all of this to do with abuse? Just this – abusive people love to pile false guilt upon their victims, convincing them that the bad things that happen are their fault. The direct result of the victim's own behavior. And worse, many times Christians affirm that this is true. If the victim will behave "better" – the abuser's actions can be improved. And the sincere Christian victim can even start to believe that if she would just be a better wife, God would be pleased with her and the abuse would lessen. In fact, she often thinks that she is the cause of most all this trouble, which is what the people around her seem to believe anyway. If God were happy with her, then her life would be better. So she tries. She accepts the guilt. She works to earn God's favor by doing better at…. you name it.

But God is not like that. In fact, God is most often in the business of giving us what we don't deserve, and that is called grace. And He withholds from us what we do deserve – that is called mercy. God loves to give His children good things. Not because He has to. Not because we have been "good." But because He is good. And that is called love.

We would all do well to examine our thinking for the magical element and reject it. Whether it be our taking on the false responsibility for an abuser's rage, or seeing that rage as punishment from the Lord because we weren't as good as we should have been. The fact is, we aren't that powerful.

# 76

# WHY KIND, GENTLE, NICE CHRISTIANS, AREN'T

*"It is actually reported that there is sexual immorality among you, and of a kind that is not tolerated even among pagans, for a man has his father's wife. And you are arrogant! Ought you not rather to mourn? Let him who has done this be removed from among you." (1 Cor. 5:1)*

ONE OF THE GREATEST SOURCES of enablement the abuser enjoys in our churches comes from what on the surface looks like the kindest, gentlest, most merciful, loving Christian in the church. In the name of "mercy and love and grace" this kind of individual reminds us frequently that

- All sinners are the same.

- All of us are just as sinful as anyone else.

- God requires us to show mercy and forgiveness to all.

- Everyone is welcome in our churches.

The single statement by the Apostle Paul above disproves every single one of these notions. Notice his points very carefully:

- The Corinthians were sinning in a shocking way by permitting this man to continue in their church.

- This man's sin was so shocking that not even pagans would tolerate it.

- The Corinthians were not showing this man mercy and love; rather they were motivated by sinful arrogance, boasting about how broad-minded they were.

- It was a sad, mournful situation bringing shame to Christ's name.

Many Christians today do not like to hear about abuse and abusers in their church.

They don't like to be told that such a person is guilty of a particularly evil wickedness. They don't want to be called to put that evil out from among them. And they don't like to hear that a person who lives like an abuser simply is not and cannot be a Christian.

Consequently, they gut the gospel of any kind of requirement for repentance. They preach a cheap grace that does not necessarily transform a person's life. In their public prayers they love to announce that God loves us all, no matter what, no matter how, no matter...well, no matter. He just loves us all and in the end most everyone is a Christian who says they are a Christian. Including the abuser.

This is not kindness. It is not the gentleness of Jesus. It isn't nice. It is arrogance and it is sin, just like what Paul rebuked the Corinthians for. It is, shall we say, a false gospel. And it cruelly oppresses the weak and downtrodden.

The Bible does not teach us that God's mercy and grace are infinite. Did you hear that? Let me say it again. The Bible does not teach that God's mercy and grace are infinite. If they were, there would be no hell. But then, there would be no justice either and God would be found guilty of injustice.

*"Let him who has done this be removed from among you."*

# 77

# WHY DON'T VICTIMS OF ABUSE "JUST GET OVER IT?"

SHOULD VICTIMS OF ABUSE, if they are Christians, be able to "just get over it"? Are Christians immune to Post Traumatic Stress Disorder? Many Christians think so. I would suspect that some of our readers who have suffered abuse may have been given that advice from other believers. "Trust in Christ. Stop being depressed. Move on." Well, let's take a look at Paul's experience.

> *"Five times I received at the hands of the Jews the forty lashes less one. Three times I was beaten with rods. Once I was stoned. Three times I was shipwrecked; a night and a day I was adrift at sea; on frequent journeys, in danger from rivers, danger from robbers, danger from my own people, danger from Gentiles, danger in the city, danger in the wilderness, danger at sea, danger from false brothers; in toil and hardship, through many a sleepless night, in hunger and thirst, often without food, in cold and exposure." (2 Corinthians 11:24-27)*

The Apostle Paul suffered horrific trauma, shame, accusations, and murderous hatred. Just consider the list above. And we know this is not a complete recounting of all of his trials. His life ended in execution.

Paul was granted remarkable enablement by Christ so that he was sustained in his Apostolic calling through every hardship. It would seem that the Lord grants all of His people strength and comfort and gifting in accordance with the ministry he gives each one. Paul wrote of an amazing and unique experience:

*"I must go on boasting. Though there is nothing to be gained by it, I will go on to visions and revelations of the Lord. I know a man in Christ who fourteen years ago was caught up to the third heaven – whether in the body or out of the body I do not know, God knows. And I know that this man was caught up into paradise – whether in the body or out of the body I do not know, God knows – and he heard things that cannot be told, which man may not utter." (2 Corinthians 12:1-4)*

But even with this vision, did Paul completely escape all symptoms and effects of these traumatic events? Let him answer the question –

*"We are afflicted in every way, but not crushed; perplexed, but not driven to despair; persecuted, but not forsaken; struck down, but not destroyed; always carrying in the body the death of Jesus, so that the life of Jesus may also be manifested in our bodies." (2 Corinthians 4:8-10)*

No, Paul felt it. But the Lord sustained him through it. His faith did not fail. He was afflicted, crushed, persecuted, and struck down. Christ Himself in the Garden of Gethsemane sweat profusely in turmoil, yet submitted to the Father's will.

It is therefore a grave error – and unfortunately a common one, to think that Christians who suffer trauma, whether it be from abuse or accident or terminal illness or tragic loss, to "buck up" and get over it. Christians are strengthened by Christ so that we will never have our faith in Him destroyed, but He permits us to experience trials and traumas and their effects. Many times, even Christian victims of abuse need therapy and counseling and help from someone who really understands trauma. We should never tell a suffering Christian to just "keep on the sunny side of life."

# 78

# You Will Be Tempted to Go Back to Egypt

*"And the whole congregation of the people of Israel grumbled against Moses and Aaron in the wilderness, and the people of Israel said to them, 'Would that we had died by the hand of the LORD in the land of Egypt, when we sat by the meat pots and ate bread to the full, for you have brought us out into this wilderness to kill this whole assembly with hunger.'" (Exodus 16:2-3)*

*"But the people thirsted there for water, and the people grumbled against Moses and said, 'Why did you bring us up out of Egypt, to kill us and our children and our livestock with thirst?'" (Exodus 17:3)*

*"Then all the congregation raised a loud cry, and the people wept that night. And all the people of Israel grumbled against Moses and Aaron. The whole congregation said to them, 'Would that we had died in the land of Egypt! Or would that we had died in this wilderness! Why is the LORD bringing us into this land, to fall by the sword? Our wives and our little ones will become a prey. Would it not be better for us to go back to Egypt?'" (Numbers 14:1-3)*

I SUSPECT THAT I could simply post the verses above and most all of you would get the point without me even writing anything further. But I will.

One of the most disheartening and even frightening things that I experience (I imagine many of you have as well) when trying to help abuse victims is knowing that it is very likely that once they do leave the abuser, there is a likelihood that they will return. I think I read once that the average is something like seven "leavings" before it actually "takes". You can correct me on that if need be.

Now, I do not quote the verses above about Israel grumbling and moaning and sinning in order to guilt any victim of abuse. They were indeed sinning, but an abuse victim who gets drawn back to her (or his) abuser is, in most cases at least, not sinning against the Lord. I simply point you all to these verses as a picture of what we can expect when we leave cruel bondage. We can count on being tempted to return to it.

As we walk through these very hard cases with victims, we feel the pressure right along with them. The danger of running the gauntlet of leaving, not to mention the difficulty of finding support when so many professionals don't understand domestic abuse, can seem more scary than the danger of staying. Living with the abuser is living with the devil we know, when we leave the abuser we may encounter other snakes under other rocks that we had no expectation of meeting, but lo! they strike us when we are wanting them help us. When you leave, here are some things that can and most likely will happen:

- The abuser's rage might increase in intensity (leaving can be the most dangerous time for a victim).

- The abuser goes to work even more diligently to alienate your friends and family from you, blaming you for all marriage problems.

- A victim may find herself out of a job, out of money, wondering where she is going to live.

- Pastors and churches go to work to pressure and condemn the victim, insisting she return. She may be shunned by people she thought were her friends.

- And then the courtroom. The fear of losing child custody. Restraining orders. Legal bills.

- The abuser may seize the victim's car, taking away her only mode of transportation.

All of this and more can happen when we knock the sand off our sandals and leave Egypt. And when it does, you can be sure that the victim is going to be tempted to just give in and return to bondage.

We need to be warned in advance of these things so that when they happen we will not be taken by surprise. Something like what Jesus warned us about regarding the world:

*"I have said these things to you, that in me you may have peace. In the world you will have tribulation. But take heart; I have overcome the world." (John 16:33)*

Sometimes when we help a victim get free, we can end up on the receiving end of words rather like this:

*Then Moses turned to the LORD and said, "O Lord, why have you done evil to this people? Why did you ever send me? For since I came to Pharaoh to speak in your name, he has done evil to this people, and you have not delivered your people at all." (Ex. 5:22-23)*

Or like this:

*"They met Moses and Aaron, who were waiting for them, as they came out from Pharaoh; and they said to them, 'The LORD look on you and judge, because you have made us stink in the sight of Pharaoh and his servants, and have put a sword in their hand to kill us.'" (Ex. 5:20-21)*

I have personally had this happen. One lady, in her confusion and suffering who had poured out the details of her situation to me over a period of several months, experienced a setback when she met with the elders of her church. She was scared, and I understand that. She wrote me that night and said "Oh, I wish I had just left well enough alone. I wish I had never contacted you." I have not heard from her since.

Therefore, let's all get a very firm hold on this truth:

When a victim resolves and sets out to leave her abuser, her situation may very well initially get worse rather than better. She needs to be warned in advance so that when that thirst in the wilderness sets in and she hears Egypt beckoning her, she won't cave in.

Don't go back to Egypt. There really wasn't anything good there. It was slavery and death.

# 79

# A CORRUPT CHURCH
# OPPRESSES THE WEAK

*"Hear the word of the LORD, you rulers of Sodom! Give ear to the teaching of our God, you people of Gomorrah! "What to me is the multitude of your sacrifices? says the LORD; I have had enough of burnt offerings of rams and the fat of well-fed beasts; I do not delight in the blood of bulls, or of lambs, or of goats. 'When you come to appear before me, who has required of you this trampling of my courts? Bring no more vain offerings; incense is an abomination to me.*

*New moon and Sabbath and the calling of convocations– I cannot endure iniquity and solemn assembly. Your new moons and your appointed feasts my soul hates; they have become a burden to me; I am weary of bearing them. When you spread out your hands, I will hide my eyes from you; even though you make many prayers, I will not listen; your hands are full of blood. Wash yourselves; make yourselves clean; remove the evil of your deeds from before my eyes; cease to do evil, learn to do good; seek justice, correct oppression; bring justice to the fatherless, plead the widow's cause.'" (Isaiah 1:10-17)*

WE HAVE HERE the Lord's words to His own people, Israel, in the days of the Old Covenant. So corrupt had they become that He calls them Sodom and Gomorrah. They continued with their multitudes of sacrifices, claiming to worship the Lord faithfully, but the Lord rejects it. He sees the reality of their hearts and motives and all that their "worship" is to him is a "trampling of His courts." He commands it to cease. Their offerings are disgusting to Him. Rank iniquity and a supposed "solemn assembly" simply cannot co-exist. They stood in their worship services and spread out their hands to pray. Those same hands were covered with guilt – with the blood of the ones they had oppressed. They were doers of evil. Now notice very carefully in the Lord's command to them to repent that the "good" they needed to learn involved seeking justice, correcting oppression, bringing justice to the fatherless, and pleading the widow's cause. Isn't that interesting? This tells us that one of the most wicked evils carried out by the "church" of that day was the oppression and abuse of widows and orphans.

Therefore, as we have said in other posts on this blog, where there is injustice dealt out to abuse victims and where the abusers are allowed to remain in the assembly of the "church," spreading out their hands in "worship" each Sunday, you can be sure what the Lord thinks of the entire mess. He calls for such a church to cease from its worship and repent. It would be better for the doors of such a place to be locked shut until everyone washes themselves from evil by true repentance. The oppression of the weak, of victims, even the abuse of children is quite widespread in today's churches. Isaiah plainly tells us here what the Lord thinks of such places, AND what such "churches" truly are in reality.

# 80

# Abusers Claim to Tell Us Our Thoughts and Motives

*"For who knows a person's thoughts except the spirit of that person, which is in him? So also no one comprehends the thoughts of God except the Spirit of God." (1 Corinthians 2:11)*

*"The heart knows its own bitterness, and no stranger shares its joy. (Proverbs 14:10)*

I CAN STILL HEAR IT. "Pastor, I know why you did that." "Jeff, you always do that because….". Every single one of the abusers who have targeted me over the years have used this kind of tactic. And for a long time I believed them at least to some degree. "Yes, maybe my motive was bad? Maybe that was what I was thinking? Or was it?"

Abusers come to this evil tactic naturally. As children of the devil, they are accusers. One very effective means of controlling people is to announce to them that you are able to read their minds, to see into the very recesses of their hearts. That you know better than they themselves do what they are thinking and what their intentions are. Of course the thing is preposterous as the Scriptures above say. No matter how well we know someone, we are not capable of fully discerning their inner being.

Now, when abuser claims to read your mind and your motives, he is making this claim in order to accuse you. Notice he never uses this "ability" to compliment, but to destroy. What he allegedly sees in your mind and heart, he insists, is not good. "You did this for selfish reasons." "You were only thinking of yourself." "You were lying." "You were lusting." "You weren't even thinking." "You wanted the glory for yourself..." and on it goes.

This has become a very clear red flag sign of an abuser to me. Whenever I hear someone using this kind of tactic, I know I am at minimum dealing with an unsafe person.

When we are targeted with this kind of attack often enough, we begin to doubt our ability to even perceive and trust our own conclusions. This then is all designed to force us back under the power of the wicked because, they claim, they DO KNOW the truth. They say they can read us like a book. They say they want to "help us understand" what our thoughts and motives really are.

God's Word says the thing is a big scam. NO ONE knows a person's thoughts except the spirit of the person. Furthermore, even my own inner self person doesn't fully know myself! It takes the Spirit of the Lord in me to show me what is in me, whether good or bad. And it is to Him alone we look:

> *"Search me, O God, and know my heart! Try me and know my thoughts! And see if there be any grievous way in me, and lead me in the way everlasting!" (Psalms 139:23-24)*

# 81

# THE SPIRIT OF THE ABUSER AND THE MASS MURDERER

*"You are of your father the devil, and your will is to do your father's desires. He was a murderer from the beginning, and does not stand in the truth, because there is no truth in him. When he lies, he speaks out of his own character, for he is a liar and the father of lies." (John 8:44)*

MOST OF YOU KNOW that at the root of the abuser's mentality is his profound sense of entitlement to have power and control. Power. Control. "I will be like the Most High." That is what explains him. That is what makes him tick. On the surface he may seem very confusing and contradictory (many abusers want to keep people in the dark about who they really are what they are really up to), but when you finally realize that he is all about power and control, things begin to make sense. He is, after all, a child of that fiendish father, the devil.

Now, the devil is a murderer. Why? Because he demands power and control. He wants to be God, and therefore he lusts for the power of life and death. HE will determine who lives and who dies. And this is the very thing that makes these mass murderers do what they do. Why does someone walk into a mall, for instance, and start slaughtering people they don't even know? Power and control. "I am here. Look at me. I will now determine life and death. The cameras are on me. I want all eyes on me. Everyone must grovel before me."

And this, by the way, explains in my opinion why these sons of the devil typically commit suicide when they are done. As soon as they perceive that they have lost power and control, or are about to lose it (i.e., the police closing in), they exercise their one final defiant act of power and control. They determine that they will die and they will take their own life. No one else is going to do it.

Then they meet the living and true God and find out who really has power and control.

But here is my point. Abusers do not all go slaughter masses of people. Some do. Far too many do. They kill their wife. They kill her children. But even the ones who do not literally murder are of the same spirit as those who do. They all crave power and control and they are determined to get it in one way or another. This is why, I believe, that moment when an abuse victim leaves her abuser is a highly dangerous time to her. He sees he is about to lose power and control. He often decides to do something that "shows her who is really in charge here." That something can run from seizing all the money, sabotaging her career, or right on up to the hellish murder/suicide scenario we see in the papers every week.

Abusers share the very same spirit as mass murderers. Abuse is murder and the Lord sees it as such.

This is something then for which all of us need to be on guard as we relate to other people. Do any of them evidence signs of this satanic spirit of entitlement to power and control? What signs, as you look back in hindsight, might have been evident of the presence of this mentality in the early days of your relationship with your abuser? How did he evidence this craving for power and control, even in perhaps rather subtle ways back then?

> *"You said in your heart, 'I will ascend to heaven; above the stars of God I will set my throne on high; I will sit on the mount of assembly in the far reaches of the north; I will ascend above the heights of the clouds; I will make myself like the Most High.'" (Isaiah 14:13-14)*

238

# 82

# JESUS CHRIST ROLLS AWAY
# OUR SHAME

*"And the LORD said to Joshua, "Today I have rolled away the reproach of Egypt from you." And so the name of that place is called Gilgal to this day." (Joshua 5:9)*

SHAME IS A SUBJECT that we all need to devote considerable effort to study and understand, especially in regard to how it is working its evil in us. And yet I am finding that it is also a subject that we want to avoid. But avoiding any "hurtful way in us" is never a good idea. To do so is like denying cancer that the doctor shows us in there.

I recently preached a sermon on the 5th chapter of Joshua, and I specifically zeroed in on verse nine, quoted above. This verse really struck me as I prepared the sermon and thought about what "the reproach of Egypt" was for the Israelites. One of the most glorious aspects of the gospel is contained in this verse: that in Jesus Christ, God has "rolled away" our shame. To the extent that we understand this, we will thrive. To the degree that we miss it, we will continue to be (very unnecessarily) in bondage to shame.

The reproach of Egypt concerned the history of the Israelites. They had been nothings to the Egyptians – slaves, Hebrew foreigners. Once the Pharaoh who "knew not Joseph" came to power, the Jews were abused horribly and oppressed with hard, hard labor. Any complaint on their part was met with royal contempt and their lot just grew worse. Try to imagine being a slave and in such a condition. For centuries! Your entire identity and heritage would be one of shame and reproach.

And then, after the first generation of disobedient Israelites had all perished in the wilderness, a success story finally appears. The new leader Joshua oversees a believing band of spies whose efforts are blessed, and they come back with a good report. The Lord re-establishes His covenant with them through a renewal of the sign of that covenant – circumcision, and then the Passover is observed. The Lord had caused the dread and fear of the Israelites to sweep over the fearsome inhabitants of Canaan and Jericho was about to go down after a miraculous crossing of the Jordan River (a repeat of the Red Sea crossing).

And then comes this remarkable pronouncement:

*"Today I have rolled away the reproach of Egypt from you."*

They even named the place for it; "Gilgal" means "rolling." And what was rolled away? The reproach/shame of Egypt.

I suggest to you that through abuse, we have all been shamed. Everyone has been shamed in this sinful world, and all of us have shamed others (as Sandra Wilson puts it, "Hurt People Hurt People"). But abusers are masters at shaming their victims, convincing them that they are worthless in the sight of everyone else. Being verbally abused for years, being the victim of emotional and psychological evil, being sexually abused .... and the list goes on.... instills intense shame in a person. Add to the mix the fact that we all enter this world as sinners and have plenty of history to be ashamed of at our own hands, and you have a paralyzing load of shame to pack around.

Jesus Christ endured "shame and scoffing rude," as the hymn writer put it. "In our place condemned He stood." Have you ever thought about this aspect of the cross of Christ? Why was it necessary for him to be mocked and humiliated in the hours leading up to the crucifixion? Why was He stripped naked and why the crowds of mockers taunting Him? If His mission was to come and die, then why didn't He just die? There are lots of reasons because the cross was a remarkably complex event in which many prophecies were fulfilled and Old Testament types (symbols) were brought to pass. But I think that another reason for the time frame was that on the cross and even leading up to it, Jesus Christ was mocked and scorned for us. He did indeed bear our shame. He took our reproaches.

> *"He was despised and rejected by men; a man of sorrows, and acquainted with grief; and as one from whom men hide their faces he was despised, and we esteemed him not. Surely he has borne our griefs and carried our sorrows; yet we esteemed him stricken, smitten by God, and afflicted. But he was wounded for our transgressions; he was crushed for our iniquities; upon him was the chastisement that brought us peace, and with his stripes we are healed." (Isaiah 53:3)*

I recommend to you that Jesus Christ makes this very same pronouncement to us today as He made to Joshua and the Israelites so long ago. "Today I have rolled away the reproach of Egypt from you." That is to say, when we come to faith and repentance in Christ, all of the old load of shame is rolled off of our backs. Because that person we used to be has died and a new creation has been raised up. We are not what we used to be, and we are no longer slaves to Satan. We are adopted as sons of God, made heirs of all that heaven can offer, objects of God's love, free of all condemnation...and the list goes on.

Jesus Christ is the remedy for shame. Even as we suffer as Christians, He remains the remedy for shame. He is in the business of rolling away that old sense of worthlessness. And so it is a great error if we turn to other means in efforts to deal with our shame. None of those old self-made, self-protective mechanisms (perfectionism, isolationism, etc) can work. But if we will simply turn to God's Word and carefully listen to what He says about who we are in Christ, and believe it — we will find the reproach of Egypt being rolled right off of our shoulders. It is not a one-time fight. We are going to have to battle and rebuke the shaming words and actions of the world, the devil, and of our own sinful flesh every day. But the remedy is always the same and it always works. Jesus Christ has borne our shame and rolled it all away. Minnie Steele the hymnwriter, had it right (1908) –

*I remember when my burdens rolled away;*
*I had carried them for years, night and day.*
*When I sought the blessed Lord,*
*And I took Him at His word,*
*Then at once all my burdens rolled away.*

*I remember when my burdens rolled away;*
*That I feared would never leave, night or day.*
*Jesus showed to me the loss,*
*So I left them at the cross;*
*I was glad when my burdens rolled away.*

*I remember when my burdens rolled away,*
*That had hindered me for years, night and day.*
*As I sought the throne of grace,*
*Just a glimpse of Jesus' face,*
*And I knew that my burdens could not stay.*

*I am singing since my burdens rolled away;*
*There's a song within my heart night and day.*
*I am living for my King,*
*And with joy I shout and sing:*
*"Hallelujah, all my burdens rolled away!"*

# THE TRICKLE-DOWN NATURE
## OF LEGALISM

*"But when Cephas came to Antioch, I opposed him to his face, because he stood condemned. For before certain men came from James, he was eating with the Gentiles; but when they came he drew back and separated himself, fearing the circumcision party. And the rest of the Jews acted hypocritically along with him, so that even Barnabas was led astray by their hypocrisy." (Galatians 2:11-13)*

PAUL'S LETTER TO THE GALATIANS has a lot to say about legalists. They are false teachers bringing their false gospel into the ranks of local churches with a very intentional method and motive. They distort the gospel to "trouble" us (1:7). They come into our churches in order "spy out our liberty" which we have in Christ:

*"Yet because of false brothers secretly brought in – who slipped in to spy out our freedom that we have in Christ Jesus, so that they might bring us into slavery..." (Galatians 2:4)*

*"They make much of you, but for no good purpose. They want to shut you out, that you may make much of them." (Galatians 4:17)*

*"It is those who want to make a good showing in the flesh who would force you to be circumcised, and only in order that they may not be persecuted for the cross of Christ.*

*For even those who are circumcised do not themselves
keep the law, but they desire to have you circumcised that
they may boast in your flesh." (Galatians 6:12-13)*

Let me try to show you how these verses describe the "trickle-
down" effect or "chain-of-command" of the infectious leaven of
legalism that we must constantly be on guard against. Legalistic
adherence to man-made traditions which are paraded as "God's
Word" always result in people being abused and in abusers being
enabled. (Case in point: the Pharisees).

1. A body of religious, extra-biblical tradition is created
   by man and foisted upon people as God's Word
   (indulgences, purgatory, no divorce for any reason,
   willful subjection to suffering is redemptive, etc., etc.)
   This tradition is equated with the gospel in its
   supposed redemptive power. It is what Paul calls
   "law." It can only condemn, kill, and curse.

2. This body of man-made false-gospel enslaving tradition
   becomes the foundation of a false "church." The
   power and control and authority of those who are the
   "biggies" in this false system energetically teach these
   traditions and demand adherence by all to them. And
   so the leaven begins to trickle down as "certain men
   come from James" to local churches (personally, or via
   books or podcasts or conferences, and so on).

3. Leaders in churches, impressed with the razzle-dazzle
   (i.e., power) of these big cheezers oooh and aaah at
   their false gospel teachings and take those teachings
   back to their churches. These local leaders are not only
   motivated by a lust for some personal glory, but by
   fear. Fear of what? More like, fear of "whom." Namely,
   fear of the self-appointed celebrity head honchos who
   demand circumcision (no divorce, warped views of
   headship and submission, you all know what's on this
   list). Look at Gal 6:12-13 above again. If a local pastor
   does not toe the company line, he is going to be
   ostracized and persecuted AND the numbers of people

in his church aren't going to grow (he won't be able to "boast in your flesh"). How desperately we NEED Paul's attitude today in this respect – Galatians 2:6 And from those who seemed to be influential (what they were makes no difference to me; God shows no partiality) – those, I say, who seemed influential added nothing to me.

4. So now the leaven has trickled down to the Peters (the supposed big names) and then trickle, trickle it goes down to Barnabas (let's equate Barnabas to the local church leaders). Barnabas was a good man. Son of encouragement and all that. But Paul says that EVEN Barnabas got all carried away in this hypocrisy and the infection quickly spread. He starts indicating by his behavior that the gospel is not by faith alone, but is by works of the law.

5. And so, it would go trickling, trickling, trickling (as it was doing in the churches of Galatia) into the thinking of all the people in the churches. AND THEN IT BEGINS TO TRICKLE BACK UPSTREAM TO THE TOP! What I mean is, it is self-perpetuating. As the churches embrace the tradition, the cheezers at the top level are empowered all the more. It is indeed, the classic vicious cycle.

What does this infection do? It enslaves people, it severs us from the grace of joy and freedom that is ours in Christ, it puts us into fear, and it enables abusers. How? Well, as Paul explains in Galatians, the motive of purveyors of man-made tradition and legalism is that THEY be exalted by us. Their legalism effects this exaltation (and our slavery) because these yeast-spreaders (manure spreaders) become our "Bible." THEY are the ones who tell us the tradition of God. THEY are the ones we begin to fear if we step out of line. So, we follow their rules and we give glory to them, instead of to Christ. We end up living in the fear that we used to be slaves to. "What will so and so think? Will this make them angry? I'd better go ask them…" and on and on. There are many "popes" you see. Sadly it seems that almost every local church has one.

Abusers love this because a legalistic religious environment is fertile soil for abuse. Man-made tradition by its very nature abuses people, enslaves them, and creates an environment that glories in power and control. The very thing Jesus abhorred and said that such a thing was NOT characteristic of His kingdom.

I fear that this trickling down has been going on for a long, long, long time in our churches and in the circles of evangelicalism (by that term I mean Christians who profess to believe faith alone, Christ alone, and the other solas). It is one of the chief reasons that abuse is so commonly present in the pews today. In the environment of power, people begin to share the very same mentality of abuse.

We desperately need Apostle Pauls (you don't really need to be a formal apostle to do this) to stand up "in the presence of all" and shout – "Peter! What the heck are you doing? Stop that right now! Barnabas, I am ashamed of you, of all people, getting caught up in this nonsense. We have all been crucified in Christ, and it is no longer we who live, but Christ who lives in us. And this new life that we now live, we live entirely by FAITH alone in Christ alone, who loved us and gave Himself for us. We are justified and set right with God by faith in the finished – FINISHED – work of Jesus Christ. We are sons of Abraham and heirs of the Promise God made to him 430 years before the law ever came. Jew or Gentile, slave or free, male or female – doesn't matter! Now pick up your plate and silverware and "git urself back over the Gentile table and load up on some more of that ham."

And if anyone doesn't like that, well they can just go take their legalism and tradition and go cut themselves off with it.

And that is the holy word of the Lord! Yep. Oh yes, Peter and Barnabas listened. Good for them.

# 84

# CHILDREN AND ABUSE

*"Fathers, do not provoke your children to anger, but bring them up in the discipline and instruction of the Lord." (Ephesians 6:4)*

*"Whoever receives one such child in my name receives me, (6) but whoever causes one of these little ones who believe in me to sin, it would be better for him to have a great millstone fastened around his neck and to be drowned in the depth of the sea." (Matt 18:5-6)*

AS WE HAVE DISCUSSED the nature, use, and abuse of power, authority, and control, we have learned that how a person exercises power over those who are weaker than they is a direct revelation of the real character of that person – whether good or evil. So, it is not surprising that evil people are shown up for who they really are in connection with their manner of dealing with their children.

Children are the weakest members of society. Listen to M. Scott Peck on this:

*"The most typical victim of evil is a child. This is to be expected, because children are not only the weakest and most vulnerable members of our society, but also because parents wield a power over the lives of their children that is essentially absolute. The dominion of master over slave is not far different from the domination of parent over child. The child's immaturity and resulting dependency mandate its parents' possession of great power but do not*

*negate the fact that this power, like all power, is subject to abuse of various degrees of malignancy."* [17]

Abuse victims know far more than they would ever choose to know about how power in the hands of the abuser oppresses children. It is one thing for any of us to suffer at the hands of a wicked person, but quite another to see our children suffering so. As long as loving parents and their children live, even after those children have grown into adulthood, moms and dads share in the suffering and hardship experienced by their sons and daughters. And this is how it should be. It is the nature of genuine love to rejoice with those who rejoice and weep with those who weep. But when a mother, for example, not only lives in fear of an abusive husband herself but must also witness her children being abused, the intensity of her suffering increases in proportion to her love for those children. It is not surprising that the crisis point at which an abuse victim so often resolves to leave her abuser is precipitated by a "final straw" in the abuser's evil toward her children.

Power in the hands of an evil person or regime always works its wickedness upon the weak and helpless. It is to be expected then that wherever we see children being mistreated, we will surely find a malevolent force in possession of power. Recently, the 40-year anniversary of 9 year old Kim Phuc's terrible trauma during the Vietnam War was reached. The prize-winning photo of her running from the napalm says it all. It is the weak – the children – who suffer the most. (Kim Phuc survived by the way, and is now 49 years old. The turning point in her life came when she happened upon a Bible after years and years of despair that almost led her to suicide).

God's Word leaves us with two anchors of truth in this regard:

1. The Lord will effect perfect and unfailing justice upon evil people who oppress the weak and refuse to repent. Scripture promises particularly harsh wrath

---

[17] M. Scott Peck, *People of the Lie*

against those who oppress the "little ones." Let no one who abuses children think that God does not see all of what they are doing, nor that He will fail to call them to account for it.

2.  Christ is a restorer of those who have been abused. While abuse effects great harm upon children, those who will turn to Christ and seek His redemption will unfailingly find healing. The best thing a mother can do for her children is to follow Christ herself and point them to Him.

# 85

# CHALLENGING THE NO DIVORCE FOR ABUSE FORTRESS

I CONTINUE TO HAMMER on this business of abuse as grounds for divorce because frankly I see it as the non-negotiable issue in this battle against abuse and abusers hiding in the church and being enabled by pastors and Christians. As long as anyone refuses to acknowledge that a victim of abuse has a right before God to divorce their abuser, then injustice is still going to be perpetrated by them against victims. They will keep right on insisting that victims remain in cruel bondage in Egypt.

> *"When a man sells his daughter as a slave, she shall not go out as the male slaves do. If she does not please her master, who has designated her for himself, then he shall let her be redeemed. He shall have no right to sell her to a foreign people, since he has broken faith with her. If he designates her for his son, he shall deal with her as with a daughter. If he takes another wife to himself, he shall not diminish her food, her clothing, or her marital rights. And if he does not do these three things for her, she shall go out for nothing, without payment of money."* *(Exodus 21:7-11)*

> *"But if the unbelieving partner separates, let it be so. In such cases the brother or sister is not enslaved. God has called you to peace." (1 Corinthians 7:15)*

A Christian woman was married to a wicked man for 25 years. Although the husband had vowed to love and cherish her until death parted them, he never did. His abuse of his wife might be called mere passivity. He just did not care. He was not available for a real relationship, focused himself on his own pleasures, ate the meals she cooked with unthankfulness and assumed he was as good as the next guy.

Is this abuse? "Well, yes." Does this man's wife have biblical grounds to divorce him? "Well, no," you say? "No adultery. No desertion = no divorce. It's that simple."

Then let me complicate it for you.

A Christian woman was married to a wicked man for 25 years. He too had vowed to love and cherish her until death parted them, but neither did he. He was more active in the abuse of his beloved. He regularly used cutting words until her sense of self had almost died. He mocked her efforts to beautify the home and told her she was a pathetic mother (though he never lifted a hand to help with either the house or the children). Well, at least with the unpleasant aspects of child-rearing, like discipline or helping with schooling. He was not a drunk. He went to work regularly, but he controlled and begrudged every dollar she spent. And sometimes he would rage. Throw things. Smash a wall. Scream and yell about how stupid she was to do...whatever.

Is this abuse? "Well, yes, of course it is!" Does this man's wife have biblical grounds to divorce him? "Hmmmm....no. No adultery. No desertion. No divorce. Still pretty simple." And would you be willing to explain that to her? That GOD has bound her to this man and that if she divorces him she will be guilty of a most heinous sin? "Boy, that wouldn't be easy, but I would have to do it. What God says about all of this is really very plain."

Let me muddy up the waters for you some more then.

A Christian woman was married to a wicked man for 12 years. He turned from his vows to love and cherish her just about the time they left the church after the wedding ceremony. The honeymoon was actually a crime of rape. Three months later he choked her almost unconscious in a rage over, what was it now – his beer being warm. He told her that if she ever called the police on him he would kill her. You could write the script of the next

11+ years of hell, after which this woman barely knew who she was and she wondered – how can God let this happen to me and my children? Why doesn't He send someone – a rescuer? But, of course, her Christian friends all reminded her many times that God hates divorce and that since all of us are sinners, she needed to look closely at herself to see where her faults were that contributed to the marriage "problems."

It was in the 12th year of this marriage that final events occurred. Having realized that she just could not permit her children to be exposed to this evil man any longer, she resolved to leave. She developed a plan that would involve telling her husband in a public place that she was taking the children and leaving him that day. And so she did. She picked a restaurant. She and the two girls and their father ate a meal first – it had been a normal "walk on eggshells" day – after which this brave lady told him of her decision. After staring at her with those familiar cold eyes for what seemed like forever, he got up, went outside, and she thought it was over.

It wasn't. He returned with a shotgun – right there in the restaurant – and without saying a word or making a sound, pumped a shotgun blast into each one of them. Just as coolly, it seemed, he turned and walked out. He was arrested and put in jail later that same day. The wife alone survived, though it was months before she recovered from her physical wounds. The other wounds, well – that is another story.

Is this abuse? "But of course! And of the most devilish kind!" Does this poor lady have grounds to divorce this beast called her husband? That is to say, what does God command her? I'm sorry, I can't hear you very clearly. Could you speak up? Does this lady have biblical grounds to divorce this 'man?' Didn't God say that the slave wife could go free from the marriage if her husband failed to provide food, clothing, and marital rights? Is murdering children and nearly killing their mother not a rather clear example of failing to provide life? So what do you say? What are you going to tell this lady? Does she have a right to divorce this murderer? And if your answer is no, then are you going to be the one to tell her so? Are you going to tell her that if she divorces the murderer of her children that she is guilty before God and that you will be forced to announce her sin to her church?

> *"And Jesus responded to the lawyers and Pharisees, saying, 'Is it lawful to heal on the Sabbath, or not?' But they remained silent. Then he took him and healed him and sent him away. And he said to them, 'Which of you, having a son or an ox that has fallen into a well on a Sabbath day, will not immediately pull him out?' And they could not reply to these things." (Luke 14:3-6)*

# 86

# STOP PITYING THE WICKED

*"Your eye shall not pity him, but you shall purge the guilt of innocent blood from Israel, so that it may be well with you." (Deuteronomy 19:13)*

*"They close their hearts to pity; with their mouths they speak arrogantly." (Psalm 17:10)*

*"Let there be none to extend kindness to him, nor any to pity his fatherless children!" (Psalm 109:12)*

*"Therefore, as I live, declares the Lord GOD, surely, because you have defiled my sanctuary with all your detestable things and with all your abominations, therefore I will withdraw. My eye will not spare, and I will have no pity." (Ezekiel 5:11)*

*"Moved with pity, he stretched out his hand and touched him and said to him, 'I will; be clean.'" (Mark 1:41)*

IF YOU HAVE STUDIED or experienced firsthand the tactics of the abuser, you already know that one of his favorite ploys is to play the victim and seek our pity. He has a virtual endless repertoire of variations on this scheme, because it works. He pulls it off repeatedly. How many times have you been sucked into this trap, resolving that you will never feel sorry for him again, then you turn right around and do it again? That has happened to me more than once.

Abusers do this in a split second without even having to sort it out first in their heads. They attack, then they transform into a pity-seeking "victim." One time after I had become wiser about all this, I confronted such a person. "You stop that!" I said. "Stop what? What do you mean?" "You just made a false accusation against Joe over here and when he confronted you, you pretended like you were the offended party. Stop it! We don't buy that trick here anymore." He of course continued to act clueless.

We have had to deal with people who were abusive and who regularly and actively tried to work their evil on us, and when we sat them down they looked up with those glistening "poor me" eyes like that cat in Shrek. "Oh, I just feel so nervous and threatened right now by you all." Yeah, right. The pity play.

So, what happens frequently if not normally in the church is that the wicked who play this game GET the pity while their victims get kicked around, or out. Christians very often get pity wrong in other words.

You will notice in the above scripture verses that there are times when the Lord Himself has NO pity and there are other times when His pity abounds. This is how it is to be with us if we are His people and reflect His character. We are to have NO pity on the wicked, unrepentant, deceiving worker of evil and we are to have hearts filled to overflowing with pity for the oppressed.

Don't you think it is well past time for the church to start getting pity right?

Note: The next article also addresses this subject of the abuser's quest for our pity. It is a very important subject.

# 87

# ABUSERS USE PITY AS A SNARE

*"But if anyone hates his neighbor and lies in wait for him and attacks him and strikes him fatally so that he dies, and he flees into one of these cities, then the elders of his city shall send and take him from there, and hand him over to the avenger of blood, so that he may die. Your eye shall not pity him, but you shall purge the guilt of innocent blood from Israel, so that it may be well with you."*
*(Deuteronomy 19:11-13)*

Let me apply this Scripture by paraphrasing it a bit:

*If anyone hates his wife and sets traps for her and attacks her and strikes her so that her health is ruined and over time she sees herself dying, and he runs off to another church, the elders of his first church shall contact the elders of the church to which he has fled and he shall be put out of both churches, handed over to the Lord for the destruction of his flesh. You shall not pity him, but you shall purge your church from him, lest your entire church share in the guilt of innocent blood, so that the Lord will bless you and it might be well with you.*

YOU SHALL NOT PITY HIM! To pity him is to keep him in your midst, and in doing so everyone in that church stands guilty before the Lord of the wicked man's evil! How many churches today are guilty then before the Lord? How many have innocent blood on their hands because they are harboring and enabling the wicked?

*You shall not pity him!* Abusers use pity. They use pity to manipulate us. Tricking us into pitying them is one of the tactics they use to keep up their disguise. How many of our readers have told us this? Many! "He pointed a gun at me. He abused me for years and years. But he went to church every Sunday and wept and wailed and prayed and raised his hands up in 'worship' and everyone thought he was such a godly man. Then, when I left him, he wept and wailed and raised his hands some more, and the people all came over to him in his pew and put their hands on the poor, poor godly man and prayed for him as he 'suffered' the grief of having lost his beloved, yet heartless wife." The thing is sickening and putrid, but it happens over and over again.

*You shall not pity him*! Stop it! Stop pitying the wicked. He wants you to pity him. He knows that pity is one of his most powerful means of winning you as his ally and turning you against his victim. If you pity him, you will enable him. You will be siding with him, and you will be guilty of innocent blood before God!

The 69th Psalm is messianic. These words are a prophecy of the Lord Jesus Christ suffering on the cross. But they also speak of the abuse victim, describing her painful plight very accurately:

> *"Reproaches have broken my heart, so that I am in despair. I looked for pity, but there was none, and for comforters, but I found none." (Psalm 69:20)*

Understand the irony? The one we should pity, finds no pity. The one the Lord commands us not to pity, is pitied. Pity the righteous and the Lord will bless you. Pity the unrighteous and He will be against you.

Most local churches stand under divine indictment today. They pity the wicked man, and they harden themselves against the righteous who are oppressed by the wicked. This means necessarily that most churches do not have the Lord's blessing upon them. Did you hear that? *Most local churches do not have the Lord's blessing upon them, because they pity the wicked.*

We do have One however, who hears our cry. The One who has no pity for the wicked, has treasures of pity for the righteous:

*"May all kings fall down before him, all nations serve him! For he delivers the needy when he calls, the poor and him who has no helper. He has pity on the weak and the needy, and saves the lives of the needy. From oppression and violence he redeems their life, and precious is their blood in his sight." (Psalm 72:11-14)*

# Perpetuating Traditions of
# Men as the Word of God

*"Let the prophet who has a dream tell the dream, but let
him who has my word speak my word faithfully. What has
straw in common with wheat? declares the LORD. Is not
my word like fire, declares the LORD, and like a hammer
that breaks the rock in pieces? Therefore, behold, I am
against the prophets, declares the LORD, who steal my
words from one another. Behold, I am against the
prophets, declares the LORD, who use their tongues and
declare, 'declares the LORD.'" (Jeremiah 23:28-31)*

The prophets steal words from one another. That is what was
going on in Jeremiah's day and it is what is happening commonly
in our day. And the result? Abusers and the wicked are encouraged
to remain in the churches, continuing on in their evil, not being
exposed or called to repentance. This is a subject I have written
about several times, but we cannot be reminded of it too often.

What is this "stealing of words?" Notice that the Lord says
specifically that these false preachers "steal MY words from one
another." I think what He means is not that they are at all
preaching His Word but in fact are claiming that what they are
preaching is His Word. They say, "the Lord declares" as they
preach what they have taken from another one of their kind.

I conclude that this is exactly what Jesus was talking about:

*"But you say, 'If anyone tells his father or his mother,
'What you would have gained from me is given to God, he*

*need not honor his father.' So for the sake of your tradition you have made void the word of God. You hypocrites! Well did Isaiah prophesy of you, when he said: 'This people honors me with their lips, but their heart is far from me; in vain do they worship me, teaching as doctrines the commandments of men.'" (Matthew 15:5-9)*

The commandments of men being taught as the doctrine of God! There it is. The prophets in Jeremiah's day were listening to and maybe even reading up on what this prophet and that prophet said, grabbing onto the parts they really liked, and perpetuated that teaching on the people, stamping on the label "so declares the Lord." The stole words from one another. They did not get their word from the Lord.

And that is exactly what is happening far and wide today in Christendom.

"Have you read so and so's new book? Wow! Look at what he says here about marriage and divorce!" Hey, here's another one that's really cool! You just gotta get this in your library!" And as the preachers today devour a steady diet of this stuff, often written by "Christian celebrities," the traditions of men replace the Word of God in the pulpit. The preachers steal words from one another, rather than obtaining them from the Holy Scriptures. Trite, pithy statements coined by the wordsmiths become common currency in the pulpits. The people, hearing these things presented in an authoritative, "holy" manner each Sunday, assume they must be God's Word.

*"How can you say, 'We are wise, and the law of the LORD is with us'? But behold, the lying pen of the scribes has made it into a lie." (Jeremiah 8:8)*

And the wicked love it so. Why? Because the traditions of man do not possess the power of God. Straw is being fed to the people, not wheat. The fire and the hammering of God's true Word are extinguished and softened so that the wicked no longer feel the heat or the blow. The abuser remains unmolested. The wicked thrive in "church." And God's people languish.

I did not make a conscious decision to stop reading so many books as I used to. But it has happened. To some degree every pastor is a lover of books, and that is a good thing. But if I immerse myself in the writings of men, and especially if I immerse myself in the writings of the current day's popular authors in Christendom, a very real danger looms. The tendency, even an unconscious tendency, to preach man's word and present it as God's Word, is almost a certainty. And as most of us know from sad and painful experience, when a pastor starts quoting his favorite authors with regularity in his sermons, his sermons become the straw that not only fail to feed God's people, they can begin to lead the people into enslavement and bondage. "John Piper says.....Douglas Wilson concludes....the new War Room movie teaches...." – understand? The preachers steal "God's Word" from one another rather than declaring the Word of the Lord.

# 89

# THE DANGER OF STAYING IN SPIRITUAL DIAPERS

*"About this we have much to say, and it is hard to explain, since you have become dull of hearing. For though by this time you ought to be teachers, you need someone to teach you again the basic principles of the oracles of God. You need milk, not solid food, for everyone who lives on milk is unskilled in the word of righteousness, since he is a child. But solid food is for the mature, for those who have their powers of discernment trained by constant practice to distinguish good from evil." (Hebrews 5:11-14)*

BABIES ARE RATHER helpless creatures. Especially human babies. And they stay that way for quite a long time. It is the task of faithful parents to raise those babies up to maturity so that they can feed themselves, support themselves, and hopefully, not wear diapers anymore. One sure mark of maturity is coming to a place in life in which we see selfishness progressively fading away. Another mark is developing the ability to see a wolf, to discern truth from lies.

As in the days of the Apostle to the Hebrews, many Christians today are still in diapers sucking on a bottle. They are self-centered and they are foolish and gullible to deception. They are in an incredibly dangerous position.

If the Christian is going to be able to stand against deception, he or she must grow up. Most readers here understand, at least in part, how deceptive and cunning and even charming abusers can be. We have discussed the "fog" of abuse in other articles and many of you have told your stories of many years in confusion of mind. Other readers are still in the process of coming out of that fog. And as we see the deception for what it is, we simultaneously are growing in the truth of Christ. We see the lies for what they are, but only because we are seeing the truth of God's Word as never before and "connecting the dots" by correcting one lie after another with the Word of God. We are learning to use the armor of Christ: the shield of faith, the breastplate of righteousness, the sword of the Spirit and so on. Flaming missiles are shot at us, but we are intercepting more and more of them before they can do their damage. We are taking every thought captive, increasingly, to Christ –

> *"For the weapons of our warfare are not of the flesh but have divine power to destroy strongholds. We destroy arguments and every lofty opinion raised against the knowledge of God, and take every thought captive to obey Christ..." (2 Corinthians 10:4-5)*

Now, all of this growing up takes the Spirit of God working in us to apply the Word of God and transform our minds. BUT, it also requires effort on our part. Lots of effort. It requires diligent prayer, diligent study of Scripture, and diligent use of other means of grace such as fellowship with other believers, including pastors and teachers given by God to equip us:

> *"And he gave the apostles, the prophets, the evangelists, the shepherds and teachers, to equip the saints for the work of ministry, for building up the body of Christ, until we all attain to the unity of the faith and of the knowledge of the Son of God, to mature manhood, to the measure of the stature of the fullness of Christ, so that we may no longer be children, tossed to and fro by the waves and carried about by every wind of doctrine, by human cunning, by craftiness in deceitful schemes. Rather, speaking the truth in love, we are to grow up in every way into him who is the head, into Christ, from whom the*

*whole body, joined and held together by every joint with which it is equipped, when each part is working properly, makes the body grow so that it builds itself up in love."* *(Ephesians 4:11-16)*

Many of you faithfully gave yourselves to the fellowship of believers in your churches and sat under the teaching ministry of pastors. And then you were shamefully treated, and in some cases put out of your churches through the deceptions of your abuser and the ignorance of the church. But you must not permit that experience to stop your use of every means of grace you can to facilitate your continued growth into maturity in Christ. We are surrounded with massive amounts of wonderful resources. In addition to the Scriptures, which must remain our primary object of study, we have classic Christian books that faithfully represent God's Word. Take the works of J.C. Ryle for example, which can be obtained very cheaply. *Practical Religion, Holiness, Light From Old Times* and *Old Paths* are just a few that in themselves will go very far in taking a Christian to maturity even during the time when a sound church is not available.

Don't be satisfied with spiritual infancy. It is a dangerous condition in which to remain. We all need to be prepared to meet that evil "angel of light" when he comes around knocking at our door and be ready to counter his wiles with the fiery hammer of the Word of God.

# 90

# TYPICAL TACTICS OF ABUSE

RECENTLY WE RECEIVED a communication from a person unknown to us. Here is the brief interaction we had. How would you handle this? What tactics do you see him using here? What is he trying to do by using these tactics with us? What is the most revealing phrase he uses that tells us what he is really up to? Oh, and why do you think he ended with "may the Lord bless you"?

Husband to Unholy Charade: "I'd really like to talk to you. My marriage is about to go through a divorce."

Unholy Charade Response: "I refer you to the resources on our Unholy Charade web page. There is a wealth of helpful info there."

Husband's Reply to Unholy Charade: "My wife is relying fully on your literature … I'd like to speak with you one on one if at all possible. We have gone thru the ringer and have had so many false people giving guidance and council [sic] and are so far away from reconciling now. If your [sic] too important to hold a phone call I fear my wife may be being lead [sic] down the wrong path yet again….".

When we told him, "No, we are not going to talk with you," here was his reply. Notice how people who crave power and control simply will not take "No" for an answer. They hate it and they just have to get in the last shot:

His Response to our "No": I've been involved in ministry for years now. There are many guys like you, for instance Joel Olsteen [sic]. Have a whole entourage and can talk a good talk but when it comes to one on one they are not capable. I don't appreciate how you turned the energy around on me but I assure you that I only came in good favor and love looking to know who we are dealing with. The evidence shows exactly that. I'm not sure if your [sic] Christian but if you are you are not displaying love at all. May the Lord bless you and help you in all your need.

This is very, very typical of the abuser, the narcissist, the sociopath/psychopath. What I mean is, this kind of a reaction they give to being told "No."

Another one, a slick sociopath I am sure, several years ago pulled this on me. He showed up at our church impeccably dressed and had all the Christianese lingo down, along with a story of having mixed it up with some relatively famous people. On just his second Sunday at our church he emailed me (that afternoon) and said he wanted to make an appointment to see me and talk about me "discipling" him. I told him that we disciple people every Sunday in our church through the classes we teach and the sermon in the worship service and that he should step up and take advantage of those. Right away he fired back an email almost identical to what this guy here in this article did – "Oh, well I see that you have no time for someone as unimportant as me."

So, this tactic is very typical of these types and we must beware of it and not yield to it.

# 91

## AN EVIL PIOUS SILENCE

*"Let not those rejoice over me who are wrongfully my foes, and let not those wink the eye who hate me without cause. For they do not speak peace, but against those who are quiet in the land they devise words of deceit." (Psalm 35:19-20)*

AS WE HAVE WRITTEN in other posts, it is very characteristic of evil people to use non-verbal means to communicate their abuse on others. One of these dastardly dark tricks is the evil man saying "I must not say anymore. I don't want to gossip." His intent with this false saintliness is to cover up, to hide truth, and to pressure others into being silent about evil as well. There is absolutely nothing saintly about such a person. He is a child of the darkness.

Let me illustrate more clearly how this works. Let's say you are discussing some evil that has come to light. Perhaps the case of a church leader or member for instance whose hidden sin has become known, at least to some. Now, wicked people share this in common – they all lead secret lives, they dwell in hidden sin, they wear a falsely pious mask. So, when some other cohort in darkness is threatened with exposure, they become very uncomfortable. And often they launch attempts to shut down any discussion, any light-shining exposure of such a fellow's wickedness. (I have known some cases when we would have to insert "she" for "he" in our discussion here).

I have seen a couple of common means by which evil ones turn off the light of exposure –

- "I just don't think I should say any more about this. I probably have already said too much." This kind of serpent-like craftiness most typically comes right after the evil man has said something like, "I think you are guilty of unforgiveness." Then, when asked to explain and expound on that accusation, the shutdown comes – "I just don't think I can say any more about this. I probably should not have said anything at all." Having effectively sown seed of accusation, he now uses a sickening "holy saintliness" to let everyone know that further discussion of the subject would be sin.

- Another way I have seen this same tactic used repeatedly is in what I will call "Agenda Control." This happens at church meetings or at denominational general assemblies. Some evil has occurred. Perhaps some notable pastor has been arrested and charged with molesting children. And right at the start of the meeting, the powerbroker(s) stands up and says something like this: "Now, we do not want our meeting to become gossiping. We want to keep things positive and edifying. Here specifically is what we are here to discuss, and we must stick to the stated agenda. If anyone wanders from it, they will forfeit the floor." So, darkness reigns you see. Any opportunity for open, up-front exposure of truth is shut down.

- Those in power in churches and other "Christian" organizations will use the same type of tactic to promote their own desires, to get the vote outcome they want, all the while making it appear like they have allowed everyone to have input. "No, we are not here tonight to discuss that issue. We are here to have this motion put before us and to vote." Anyone who would attempt to point out how sinful use of power and control has been at work in the proceedings is immediately deemed 'out of order' and their right to be heard forfeited. "We must not say too much lest we slander a brother. You need to be silent." That's how the thing goes, you see.

Domestic abusers and their allies do these very things. They plant a seed of accusation against their victim, but when the victim or anyone else seeking justice begins to expose the evil, the wicked man works to shut down discussion. "Now, you are saying too much. You are gossiping. You don't have enough facts to even bring these issues up. You need to follow my example and keep silent."

> *The real problem among us is not so much GOSSIP, as it is NOT TALKING about evil working in our midst at all!*

There have been many "Christian" books published on the evils of the tongue. Yes, the tongue can be set on fire by hell. But generally we have been taught wrongly about just what kind of person has such a tongue. We have been told that it is the victim who is bringing the crimes and evils of the abuser to light. Wrong! It is the abuser and power-lusting Diotrephes (see 3 John) who is speaking to shut down that victim.

In contrast to all this hiding and darkness that is so typical of evil, we have the command of King Jesus given to us through His Apostle. Notice His rebuke of those who were keeping quiet about (tolerating the evil of) the wicked man:

> *"It is actually reported that there is sexual immorality among you, and of a kind that is not tolerated even among pagans, for a man has his father's wife. And you are arrogant! Ought you not rather to mourn? Let him who has done this be removed from among you. For though absent in body, I am present in spirit; and as if present, I have already pronounced judgment on the one who did such a thing. When you are assembled in the name of the Lord Jesus and my spirit is present, with the power of our Lord Jesus, you are to deliver this man to Satan for the destruction of the flesh, so that his spirit may be saved in the day of the Lord. Your boasting is not good. Do you not know that a little leaven leavens the whole lump? Cleanse out the old leaven that you may be a new lump, as you*

*really are unleavened. For Christ, our Passover lamb, has been sacrificed." (1 Corinthians 5:1-7)*

One final but very important point regarding all this:

*There comes a time when anyone having knowledge of wickedness must speak out.*

Even if that speaking out means standing up and speaking 'out of order' at a church meeting or other such setting. If denomin- ational or church association leaders for instance will not provide an open platform at a general assembly or other such church meeting, then it is time to violate 'rules of order'. Like the prophets and apostles of old, and like our Lord Himself, it is time to stand up in the temple and cry out "there is wickedness here!" And then spill the beans openly even while the 'pillars' are gnashing their teeth and trying to shout you down.

Oh, and one other final thing – take care that, if you should ever see such a person standing up to expose hidden evil – take care that you do not immediately regard them as some 'troublemaker'. Many of the Lord's chosen people have done some pretty strange things to call wickedness to account.

# 92

# ANOTHER EXAMPLE OF ENSLAVING
## "BIBLICAL COUNSELING"

CHRISTIANS MUST ALWAYS FACE the threat of man-made traditions being taught as if they were the Word of God. This is how we are brought into bondage and robbed of the freedom for which Christ redeemed us (Gal 5:1ff). Preachers, church teachers, theologians, and fellow Christians confidently repeat the "company line" without ever truly thinking through what they are claiming to be the teaching of Scripture. We are commanded to be diligent and careful in our study and application of God's Word, workmen in the field of Scripture that will not have to be ashamed when Christ comes. We are to "cut it straight" as Paul told Timothy. Yet today we often see more jagged ripping than straight cutting.

When we hear some pastor or "biblical" counselor confidently make assertions, telling us that we are bound before God to do or to not do...whatever, we need to be very careful that it really is God's command and not that of man. Today I heard just such an example of a counselor/pastor making this kind of statement that, in my opinion, is not biblical and will most certainly bring the oppressed into further bondage at the hands of the wicked. Here is the statement taken from this fellow's blog:

> *"As counselors we often come across counselees who are lax in keeping their commitments. A successful and capable woman who is married to a lazy selfish man may realize that she could find a better husband. A father who promises to attend an event with his son on a Saturday, only to be offered great seats at the big game at the last*

*minute, may be tempted to abandon his commitment to his son in order to take the better offer...Expect to do some difficult things for the sake of keeping your commitments. There will be times when you may regret having made a promise but must still keep it. The capable woman with the lazy husband made a commitment before God, and she must keep it (Matthew 19:6)."*

He is referring to Psalm 15 which reads:

*"A Psalm of David. O LORD, who shall sojourn in your tent? Who shall dwell on your holy hill? He who walks blamelessly and does what is right and speaks truth in his heart; who does not slander with his tongue and does no evil to his neighbor, nor takes up a reproach against his friend; in whose eyes a vile person is despised, but who honors those who fear the LORD; who swears to his own hurt and does not change; who does not put out his money at interest and does not take a bribe against the innocent. He who does these things shall never be moved." (Psalm 15:1-5)*

As you can see, this writer takes that phrase "who swears to his own hurt and does not change" and authoritatively announces that "the capable woman with the lazy [and selfish] husband made a commitment before God, and she must keep it." (Italics mine). He then cites Matthew 19:6 as further support:

*So they are no longer two but one flesh. What therefore God has joined together, let not man separate." (Matt. 19:6)*

There is so much wrong with this fellow's use of God's Word here that it is difficult to know where to begin. I will just make a start and number the points off:

1.  Why does he zero in on a wife who is the one who wants out of her marriage? In doing so, you see, he places the onus upon the woman to keep her marriage vow. But she IS keeping her vows! Her husband is the

one who is breaking his vows! So why has this teacher set the crosshairs on HER?

2.  The scenario is described in minimizing language. "Selfish and lazy." Now think this through very carefully. Selfish and lazy. Have you ever known a selfish and lazy man who is married? What did that selfishness and laziness look like? I can tell you. It is not merely like Huck Finn skipping school to go catfishing down at the Ol' Missisip. Oh no. Read about him further in Proverbs where he is called the "sluggard." This "selfish and lazy" man is a wicked man. He is worse than an unbeliever because he will not provide for his own. He is without empathy and expects his wife to wait upon him, grabbing any income she gets and spending it on drugs or alcohol or toys. I have another name for such a man. He is an abuser. He is abusing his wife. He has regularly, habitually, and without repentance broken his marriage covenant. And that is grounds for divorce.

3.  The writer quotes Matthew 19:6, one verse out of context, giving readers the impression that filing for divorce for any reason is to break one's vow and invoke God's displeasure. Remember, David Instone-Brewer wrote a book about the New Testament teaching (including the Old Testament and Rabbinic backdrop) on marriage and divorce. But this blog post just tosses this one verse out there as support for the position that, well, too bad lady. You married that lazy, selfish, no-good and now you are stuck with him. HE can break his vows all he wants to with impunity.

4.  The writer is well known in the "biblical counseling" movement. The nouthetic stuff that we encourage people to run from. And in this movement, there is a persistent notion that with Bible in hand a counselor can "fix" things. Fix an abuser. Fix an abusive marriage. Fix a selfish, lazy, sluggard. People in this school of counseling are extremely hesitant to just come right out and say it, abuse is biblical grounds for

divorce. To do so would bring the wrath and rejection of one's fellow counselors down upon you. So you won't find clarity in the literature of this kind of counseling.

What is the true application of this phrase in Psalm 15, *"who swears to his own hurt and does not change"*? It is this: "Mr. Sluggard, Mr. selfish, lazy, abuser of your wife, breaker of your marriage covenant, YOU will never see God's holy hill. You will not be allowed into the Lord's presence. He is going to cast you away into the outer darkness because YOU wickedly destroyed your wife and your marriage covenant. And God hates that violence."

The kind of teaching then that this article contains brings Christ's people into bondage. It enables the wicked and oppresses the innocent. *And it is all around us today in the churches, in "Christian" books, in "biblical counseling" seminars.* Everywhere.

Christian, Christ has set you free. Don't permit anyone to counterfeit God's Word with man's tradition and rob you of that freedom.

# 93

# ARE THE DAUGHTERS OF EVE STUPID?

ABUSE IS THE TEST of our theology. If our theology does not lead us to render justice and kindness to victims of abuse, and if it does not lead us to an exposure of the evil of the abuser, then our theology is deficient. It is time to go back to the Scriptures and take another look.

Abusers hiding under the facade of Christianity (and remember, those are the WORST kind of abuser), LOVE to promote the notion that women are inferior to men. One way they keep this idea going in the church is to remind women that Eve was deceived by the serpent. It was, in the end, a woman who got us into this whole mess of a fallen world. Adam jumped right onto that bandwagon right off – "it was the woman YOU gave me, Lord." Women. Can't live with 'em, and can't live without 'em. What are we gonna do? Let's blame 'em and shame 'em.

Does the Bible teach that women are stupid? Inferior to men in their very mind and nature? Well, the Apostle Paul did say –

> *"For Adam was formed first, then Eve; and Adam was not deceived, but the woman was deceived and became a transgressor." (1 Timothy 2:13-14)*

And yet, he also wrote –

> *"There is neither Jew nor Greek, there is neither slave nor free, there is no male and female, for you are all one in Christ Jesus." (Galatians 3:28)*

This much we know – at least any genuine Christian knows – God's Word never contradicts itself. God's Word is truth. And truth is always in agreement. You can't have two truths opposed to one another. Like the biblical doctrines of election and free will – they may appear to be contradictory, but they are not. The problem lies with us, not with God.

When Paul says that Adam was not deceived, THAT IS NOT A COMPLIMENT TO ADAM'S INTELLIGENCE! Eve was deceived by the devil. Adam, having been given a charge by God to rule over the garden and be God's image bearer, should have KILLED that serpent. But he didn't. When he took the fruit from his wife and ate, he did so knowingly. God held him to a higher standard. His sin was greater and it was through Adam that we all fell. He is the one the devil wanted to get at all along. Adam was the federal head (representative) of our race (Romans 5).

Now, in dealing with Scriptures like this one in 1 Timothy 2, here is what I am learning from my study of the evil nature and schemes of abusers. We cannot merely teach what a Scripture does say – we must also teach what it does not say. Let me do that in this case by giving you a recent example.

We love to hear the personal stories of abuse victims who contact us through Unholy Charade. They are heart-breaking, inspiring, and instructive. One Christian lady told us recently how much she fears being deceived and coming to believe that her husband is an abuser if in fact he is not (he shows every sign of being an abuser). We understand this. Christian wives of abusers want to please Christ. They don't want to sin. But they are confused – you all know that. Abusers confuse. They generate fog, and it takes quite some time to come out of that deception. This sister in Christ said –

*"I am a woman so I could be deceived like Eve was in the garden."*

This is commendable in that you see she truly wants to know the TRUTH. She doesn't want to buy into some kind of lie. She wants a marriage that honors Christ. She admits she is capable, like all of us, of being deceived.

But is the danger of her deception to be attributed to the fact that she is a woman? I think we can help her here. Her statement can help all of us. If she is deceived (and of course she is to one degree or another), is it because she is a woman? Isn't this amazing? Talk about a trap from the devil! Yes, victims of abusers are deceived – at least until they come out of that deception. But what is the reason for that deception? *it is because her "adam" is deceiving her with his lies.* It's not HER, it's HIM! Male survivors of abuse will also tell you how they were under a deception for so long before they saw what was happening to them. Yes, this sister in Christ could be deceived. In fact, she is deceived, again, just as every single victim of abuse is deceived until the Lord leads them out of that fog. *But she is deceived because she is married to a deceiver, not because she is a woman.*

Let's take this a step further. We all know that the conservative, Bible-believing church today is deceived, horribly deceived, about abuse and abusers and their victims. That is one of the fundamental reasons for this blog and for our books—to expose this evil in the pews. Now, who is leading our churches? Women? No. In our churches, men are pastors and elders. Men are the heads of their wives and children. We teach this. We practice this. And yet, here is this terrible, terrible mess of deception. Abusers are justified. Victims are ostracized. If we could do a survey somehow of the readers of this blog, how do you suppose the breakdown according to gender would come out? What percentage are women and what percentage are men? I think you have a general idea of the answer. Why is that? It is because women are awakening to the evil of abuse in much higher numbers than men are. Hmmmm.... that doesn't sound like the daughters of Eve are all that stupid.

This article does not even begin to answer or explain all the related issues of the Bible's teaching on the nature of men and the nature of women. I haven't even tried to do that. But this much we can say with certainty – the Bible does not teach that women are stupid because they are women, nor does it teach that men are wise because they are men. There are stupid men, and stupid women because we are sinners. There are evil men, and there are evil women but not because they are men or women.

So we encourage this sister in Christ with this – the mere fact that you have come to the point of being able to write to us, to read things like this blog, to observe the things that you are observing about your husband and what he is doing to you – tells us that you are anything but a foolish, silly, easily-deceived woman. It tells us that Christ is showing you His truth and giving you His wisdom, and He is at work even now to bring you into freedom from your bondage to a cruel taskmaster.

# 94

# ARGUMENT FOR BIBLICAL DIVORCE

*"Therefore we must pay much closer attention to what we have heard, lest we drift away from it. For since the message declared by angels proved to be reliable, and every transgression or disobedience received a just retribution, how shall we escape if we neglect such a great salvation?" (Hebrews 2:1-3)*

THE EPISTLE TO THE HEBREWS uses the word "better" numbers of times. It does so because it employs the "if the lesser is true…then the greater is true." If people were held accountable to the Old Covenant which was given through Moses, THEN surely, we are even more accountable under the New Covenant, given through Christ. You see how it works? Lesser to the greater. Here is another example –

*"It is beyond dispute that the inferior is blessed by the superior. In the one case tithes are received by mortal men, but in the other case, by one of whom it is testified that he lives. One might even say that Levi himself, who receives tithes, paid tithes through Abraham, for he was still in the loins of his ancestor when Melchizedek met him." (Hebrews 7:7-10)*

Here, the Apostle is demonstrating that the priesthood of Melchizedek (Christ) is a greater priesthood than that of Levi, because Levi (existing in "seed" form in Abraham) paid tithes to Melchizedek. If the lesser is true, then surely the greater is true. Christ's priesthood is greater.

What has all of this got to do with abuse and divorce and remarriage – our focus in this blog? Simply this:

*If Scripture allows for the abandoned party to be free from the marriage covenant when the guilty party deserts them (1 Corinthians 7), then because this "lesser" evil is grounds for divorce, the greater evil must also be grounds for divorce. And what is the greater evil? It is the abuser continuing in the "marriage" and persisting in abusing his victim. This greater evil surely gives the victim biblical grounds for divorce, because the lesser evil (literal abandonment) is biblical grounds for divorce.*

Do you see it? And how bizarre and unjust we are in the Christian church! The thing smacks of the religion of the Pharisees who strain out a gnat and swallow the camel. We are more prepared (though there are many who even refuse this) to grant as grounds for divorce – desertion – than we are for active, ongoing verbal, physical, emotional abuse! But surely the latter is the greater evil. God repeatedly uses the argument from the lesser to the greater in Scripture, and therefore we are justified in doing the same. If we strain out a gnat, then let's be sure to strain out the camel too!

# 95

# CHRISTIANS HAVE NO EXCUSE

*"For wicked men are found among my people; they lurk like fowlers lying in wait. They set a trap; they catch men. Like a cage full of birds, their houses are full of deceit; therefore they have become great and rich; they have grown fat and sleek. They know no bounds in deeds of evil; they judge not with justice the cause of the fatherless, to make it prosper, and they do not defend the rights of the needy. Shall I not punish them for these things? declares the LORD, and shall I not avenge myself on a nation such as this?" (Jeremiah 5:26-29)*

THE BIBLE SPEAKS over and over and over again to the fact that Satan and his children are always at work to infiltrate Christ's people. You have it constantly in the Old Testament and the New Testament continues these warnings. Much of the New Testament in fact was written to educate us about evil so that we can identify it and put it out of our midst. Satan came into Eden right at the start.

Here we have the Lord speaking through the prophet Jeremiah. "For wicked men are found among my people."

- What are they doing there? "...they lurk like fowlers lying in wait, they set a trap, they catch men."

- How evil are they? "...they know no bounds in deeds of evil."

- What is one of the most typical expressions of this evil in the church? "...they judge not with justice the cause of the fatherless, to make it prosper, and they do not defend the rights of the needy." In other words, they deal in the currency of injustice. Instead of defending the afflicted, they oppress them further.

The Lord sees it and He vows to punish these wicked ones.

So why do professing Christians today balk when we tell them, "You have evil abusers in your church. They are parading as saints, but here is how you can spot them"? Why do the walls go up when we tell pastors and churches these things? Why do they accuse us of exaggerating and overstating the seriousness of things? It certainly isn't because God's Word is silent on these themes.

> *"Behold, the princes of Israel in you, every one according to his power, have been bent on shedding blood. Father and mother are treated with contempt in you; the sojourner suffers extortion in your midst; the fatherless and the widow are wronged in you." (Ezekiel 22:6-7)*

"Oh, but that is all Old Testament. The church in the New Covenant is not the same." No, the true church isn't the same (and neither was it in the Old Testament era), but the visible church is. The wicked still creep in and in some cases they even take control of the entire church. Victims and the oppressed will always receive injustice at the hands of these kind.

> *"For certain people have crept in unnoticed who long ago were designated for this condemnation, ungodly people, who pervert the grace of our God into sensuality and deny our only Master and Lord, Jesus Christ." (Jude 1:4)*

And yet here again, even in response to New Testament verses like this one, professing Christians typically refuse to believe that such is the case in their church. But is not Satan always on the prowl? How do we think he is going to war against us? In some vision? Most often he is on the prowl through people who parade as Christians. Resist the devil and he will flee from you. That means there is someone who has crept in and who needs to be resisted. Abusers are classic examples.

Yes, professing church, the Lord is talking to you!

> *"How long will you judge unjustly and show partiality to the wicked? Give justice to the weak and the fatherless; maintain the right of the afflicted and the destitute. Rescue the weak and the needy; deliver them from the hand of the wicked." (Psalm 82:2-4)*

Here's one more:

> *"Finally, brothers, pray for us, that the word of the Lord may speed ahead and be honored, as happened among you, and that we may be delivered from wicked and evil men. For not all have faith. But the Lord is faithful. He will establish you and guard you against the evil one." (2 Thessalonians 3:1-3)*

See it? I mean, who are these wicked and evil men Paul needs to be delivered from? Well, they are mixed in with the "all who have faith." That is to say, these agents of the evil one are in the visible church and claim to be Christians. Our primary battle as Christians is not with the world. It is with principalities and powers who creep in among us wearing disguises made of wool.

# 96

# DIVORCE FOR ABUSE ARGUED FROM COLOSSIANS 2

I TALK A LOT ABOUT DIVORCE these days. To do so brands you in most Christian circles as a troublemaker at best, and an enemy of Christ at worst. I think that I am neither. Well, I am a trouble-maker to the extent that I trouble those who trouble victims of abuse by demanding that they have no right to divorce a spouse who is an abuser. But then, like Elijah, I hope that I can say "I have not troubled Israel, but you have."

I talk and write about divorce because this is the thing that must be acknowledged if we are going to deal justice to victims. God redeemed Israel, bringing them out of cruel enslavement to Pharaoh. He did the same for us in His Son at the cross. Exodus. Leaving. Departure. That is His way. As long as someone insists that the victim of domestic abuse has no right before God to depart that already destroyed marriage covenant, then that person still enables the wicked.

As I have been preaching through Colossians, I have been impressed that this teaching that an abuse victim is bound to their abuser is entirely inconsistent with what the Apostle Paul wrote to the Colossians. No, with what he commanded the Colossians. Here is a sample of it –

> "I say this in order that no one may delude you with plausible arguments. For though I am absent in body, yet I am with you in spirit, rejoicing to see your good order and the firmness of your faith in Christ. Therefore, as you received Christ Jesus the Lord, so walk in him, rooted and

*built up in him and established in the faith, just as you were taught, abounding in thanksgiving. See to it that no one takes you captive by philosophy and empty deceit, according to human tradition, according to the elemental spirits of the world, and not according to Christ." (Col. 2:4-8)*

*"He disarmed the rulers and authorities and put them to open shame, by triumphing over them in him. Therefore let no one pass judgment on you in questions of food and drink, or with regard to a festival or a new moon or a Sabbath. These are a shadow of the things to come, but the substance belongs to Christ. Let no one disqualify you, insisting on asceticism and worship of angels, going on in detail about visions, puffed up without reason by his sensuous mind, and not holding fast to the Head, from whom the whole body, nourished and knit together through its joints and ligaments, grows with a growth that is from God.*

*If with Christ you died to the elemental spirits of the world, why, as if you were still alive in the world, do you submit to regulations—'Do not handle, Do not taste, Do not touch' (referring to things that all perish as they are used)—according to human precepts and teachings? These have indeed an appearance of wisdom in promoting self-made religion and asceticism and severity to the body, but they are of no value in stopping the indulgence of the flesh." (Col. 2:15-23)*

A Christian is not to be taken captive. We are to be on guard for any teaching that is the invention of man and not the Word of God. We are not to permit anyone to pass judgment upon us because we will not submit ourselves to their warped "gospel" of asceticism and severe treatment of our body. And in particular, we are not to submit to systems of thought (deceptive philosophies which are not according to Christ) that seem wise and plausible at first, but which consist of "ideas hatched in the brain of man" [John Calvin's phrase] and smack of the flavor of "do not handle, do not taste, do not touch" in reference to things that all perish. In other words, legalistic rules that are applied to things like food, dress, and...marriage. Yes, marriage. It is a temporal thing, right?

And so today here we have all these teachers and Christian leaders in the church, numbers of whom are quite popular, working hard to judge us and bring us into submission to their human precepts and teachings. The command of Scripture is that we reject them. And if we follow the Apostle Paul's dealings with Peter in Galatians, we also name the person, name their error, and we do so in the presence of everyone. [When is the last time you heard "those of reputation" publicly rebuke one of their own as Paul rebuked Peter?]

Listen to Judith Herman, writing in the fourth chapter of her wonderful book, *Trauma and Recovery*. Her chapter is entitled simply, Captivity.

> *"A single traumatic event can occur almost anywhere. Prolonged, repeated trauma, by contrast, occurs only in circumstances of captivity. When the victim is free to escape, she will not be abused a second time; repeated trauma occurs only when the victim is a prisoner, unable to flee, and under the control of the perpetrator. Such conditions obviously exist in prisons, concentration camps, and slave labor camps. These conditions may also exist in religious cults, in brothels and other institutions of organized sexual exploitation, and in families.*
>
> *Political captivity is generally recognized, whereas the domestic captivity of women and children is often unseen. A man's home is his castle; rarely is it understood that the same home may be a prison for women and children. In domestic captivity, physical barriers to escape are rare. In most homes, even the most oppressive, there are no bars on the windows, no barbed wire fences. Women and children are not ordinarily chained, though even this occurs more often than one might think. The barriers to escape are generally invisible. They are*

*nonetheless extremely powerful. Children are rendered captive by their condition of dependency. Women are rendered captive by economic, social, psychological, and legal subordination, as well as by physical force. [We would add, religious subordination as well].*

*Captivity, which brings the victim into prolonged contact with the perpetrator, creates a special type of relationship, one of coercive control. This is equally true whether the victim is taken captive entirely by force, as in the case of prisoners and hostages, or by a combination of force, intimidation, and enticement, as in the case of religious cult members, battered women, and abused children. The psychological impact of subordination to coercive control may have many common features, whether that subordination occurs within the public sphere of politics or within the private sphere of sexual and domestic relations.*

*In situations of captivity, the perpetrator becomes <u>the most powerful person in the life of the victim, and the psychology of the victim is shaped by the actions and beliefs of the perpetrator.</u>" [Emphasis mine].*

Now, unless Christians who oppose divorce for abuse are willing to pronounce Judith Herman and many other professionals who have studied and researched trauma, wrong, then all they are going to be left with is two alternatives.

1. But it is different with Christians. The Christian will never let the abuser's actions and beliefs affect her. It's different for Christians." Or,

2. Being in a prison camp or concentration camp or being held captive in a basement by a criminal is different than living with and being bound to an abuser.

Neither of these options will hold water. Study and talk to Christians who have been in prolonged relationship with abusers.

Ask them to tell their stories. Have them tell you what those years of abuse did to them. Talk with them and work with them to try and help them come out of the fog and to become a person once again. No, abuse victims suffer the very same effects and in many ways they suffer even more severely than someone in a wartime prison camp. Why? Because in war, the enemy is plainly visible to all. But when it comes to the abuser, well, listen to Judith Herman again:

> *"Little is known about the mind of the perpetrator. Since he is contemptuous of those who seek to understand him, he does not volunteer to be studied. Since he does not perceive that anything is wrong with him, he does not seek help – unless he is in trouble with the law. His most consistent feature, in both the testimony of victims and the observations of psychologists, is his apparent normality. Ordinary concepts of psychopathology fail to define or comprehend him."*

Did you hear that, pastors and Christian experts on marriage and the family? Psychologists have trouble identifying and understanding these abusers! Why should we pastors or Christians or theologians be so puffed up that we claim that we can? "Well, because we have the Bible." Yes, we have the Bible. But even in light of Scripture which does indeed tell us about the psychopathology of evil and sin, we don't get it! How do I know? Because I know how miserably most church leaders deal with victims of abuse and how they are duped by the abuser.

I know that many people will disagree with me and insist that I am not handling Scripture accurately here. So be it. But the message I get from Colossians 2 is that a Christian does not need – no, a Christian must not – permit anyone to judge them or force any man-made traditions upon them that would bind them in a captivity that destroys their person, fogs their mind, and thereby necessarily distances them from Christ and brings an evil person into prominence in their every waking moment.

# BENEDICTION

*To you, O LORD, I call; my rock, be not deaf to me, lest, if you be silent to me, I become like those who go down to the pit. Hear the voice of my pleas for mercy, when I cry to you for help, when I lift up my hands toward your most holy sanctuary.*

*Do not drag me off with the wicked, with the workers of evil, who speak peace with their neighbors while evil is in their hearts. Give to them according to their work and according to the evil of their deeds; give to them according to the work of their hands; render them their due reward. Because they do not regard the works of the LORD or the work of his hands, he will tear them down and build them up no more.*

*Blessed be the LORD! For he has heard the voice of my pleas for mercy. The LORD is my strength and my shield; in him my heart trusts, and I am helped; my heart exults, and with my song I give thanks to him. The LORD is the strength of his people; he is the saving refuge of his anointed. Oh, save your people and bless your heritage! Be their shepherd and carry them forever. (Psalms 28:1-9)*

www.ingramcontent.com/pod-product-compliance
Lightning Source LLC
Chambersburg PA
CBHW022330280326
41934CB00006B/593